MORALE AND MOTIVATION

SKILLS FOR SUCCESS

LEADERSHIP:
The Key to Management Success
by L. Bittel

MANAGING YOURSELF:
How to Control Emotion, Stress, and Time
by A. Goodloe, J. Bensahel, and J. Kelly

COMMUNICATING:
How to Organize Meetings and Presentations
by J. Callanan

HIRING THE RIGHT PERSON FOR THE RIGHT JOB
by C. Dobrish, R. Wolff, and B. Zevnik

MORALE AND MOTIVATION:
How to Measure Morale and Increase Productivity
by E. Benge and J. Hickey

EUGENE BENGE
JOHN HICKEY

MORALE AND MOTIVATION

HOW TO MEASURE MORALE AND INCREASE PRODUCTIVITY

FRANKLIN WATTS

New York   London   Toronto   Sydney

Library of Congress Cataloging in Publication Data

Benge, Eugene Jackson, 1896-
Morale and motivation.

Includes index.
1. Employee morale. 2. Employee motivation.
I. Hickey, John (John V.) II. Title.
HF5549.5.M6B46   1984   658.3'14   84-11834
ISBN 0-531-09579-7

CONTENTS

PREFACE   XV

PART I

1. PREPARING A SYSTEM TO
    INCREASE WORKER PRODUCTIVITY   5
    What Is the Link between Morale and
        Productivity?   6
    What Companies Are Doing   7
    Another View of Morale Surveys   8
    Attitudes, Job Satisfaction, and Employee
        Morale   9
    Ways to Study Employee Morale   11

2. DETERMINING MORALE THROUGH
    THE UNSIGNED QUESTIONNAIRE   13
    Asking the Right Kinds of Questions   14

3. TECHNIQUES FOR ADMINISTERING
   THE QUESTIONNAIRE   26
   Explaining the Questionnaire   27
   Editing Questionnaires   28
   Administering the Questionnaire in
      Decentralized Companies   29

4. MORALE INDICES:
   HOW TO CALCULATE AND
   INTERPRET THEM   30
   Planning the Format   30
   Setting Up the Tabulation   31
      The Tally Process in Action   32
   Compiling a Morale Index   35
      Calculating Morale Indices in Percentages   36
   Using Morale Indices   37

5. ANALYZING DATA
   FROM MORALE INDICES   39
   Analyzing Percentage Findings   40
   Comparing Departments   40
   Analyzing Initial Surveys   41
   Comparisons in Action   44

6. THE VALUE OF EMPLOYEE COMMENTS   49
   Analyzing Employee Comments   51
   Selected Employee Comments   52

7. A SELECTION OF FINDINGS
   FROM 144 SURVEYS   53
      Going Outside the Company to Fill
         Vacancies   53
      Too Many Bosses   55
      The Boss Who Didn't Boss   55

Wage Inequity   55
Food for Employees   56
Resolving Conflicting Demands   56
Employee Councils   57
Unsolvable Problems   57
Community Relations   57
Overcoming Resistance to Mechanization   58
Increasing Job Satisfaction   58
Reorganizing Management   59
Enriching Jobs   59

8. RECOMMENDATIONS
    AND MANAGEMENT ACTIONS   61
    Company X Recommendations   61
    Recommendations from Surveys   63
    Implementing the Improvement Program   65
    Report to Employees   65

PART II

9. KEYS TO MOTIVATION   71
    From Coercion to Motivation   72
        Workers and Their Needs   73
        How to Determine Job Satisfaction
            Potential   74
    Criteria for Job Designs That Provide
        Motivation   74
    Obstacles to Motivation   77
        The Group as a Dynamic Force for
            Motivation   79
        Rewards and Incentives as Means of
            Motivation   80
    Training as a Motivator   81
    Motivation through Communication   82

10. THE MOTIVATING ENVIRONMENT 85
Physical Factors 86
Determining When to Make Physical
Improvements 88
Other Demotivating Conditions 89

11. THE MANAGER AS
PRIME MOTIVATOR 91
Using Psychotherapeutic Technique
to Improve Performance 91
Self-esteem as the Key 93
Empathetic Listening 94
A Wasted Asset 95
Identifying Deadwood Employees 96
The First Step: Talk It Out 97
Four Sparks of Life 98

12. MOTIVATING SPECIFIC SEGMENTS
OF THE EMPLOYEE POPULATION 100
Motivating Groups 101
Testing Your Group Awareness 102
Answers and Explanations 103
Evaluating Your Score 107

13. MOTIVATING SPECIFIC EMPLOYEES 108
Analyzing a Subordinate's Situation 110
An Actual Case 112
Taking Necessary Action 114
Motivating the Professional 115
Financial Remuneration 117
Professional Prestige 117
Motivating Your Secretary 119
Job Enrichment 120

PART III

14. THE CASE OF
    THE MOTIVATED
    PRODUCTION FACILITY:
    HEWLETT-PACKARD   127
    How Workers Describe the HP Way   128
    Providing for Worker Security   129
    The Value of Trust   130
    The Supervisor and Autonomy   130
    Rewards and Incentives   132
    Continuous Training   133
    Management by Wandering Around
       (MBWA)   134
    Freedom to Plan Work   135
    Physical Environment   136
    Motivation through Goal-Setting   138
    Caring as a Motivational Force   140

15. THE CASE OF
    THE MOTIVATED OFFICE:
    OCCIDENTAL INSURANCE   142
    Rising Clerical Costs Force Changes   143
    The Assumption of Theory Y   144
    Developing Motivation from Top Levels
       of Management Down   144
    More Clerical-Level Changes   145
    Goal-Setting for Clerical Employees   146
    Do's and Don'ts of MBO   148
    Social Responsibility as Motivation   149
    Assumption of Responsibility   151
    Make Changes Gradually   152

16. THE CASE OF ORGANIZATION FOR
    MOTIVATION: KAISER PERMANENTE   154
    Recognition of Problems   156
    Group Consideration of Problems   157
    Why This Motivational Technique
       Gets Results   158
    Measuring the Effects of Motivation   159

17. THE CASE OF A NEW METHOD
    OF MOTIVATION: QUALITY CIRCLES   161
    Quality Circles at Sperry Vickers   162
    Measuring the Results of the Quality
       Circle Method   164
    Quality Circles at International Harvester   165
    Methods of Operating Quality Circles   166
    The Role of the Facilitator   168
    Results of the Quality Circle Method   169
    Costs and Savings from Circles   170
    A Quality Circle in Action   171
    Getting Complete Information   172
    Quality Circles Motivate through
       Participation   174
    Your Involvement in Quality Circles   174
       Pitfalls to Avoid in Setting Up QCs 175
       A Checklist of Potential Problems   176

18. THE CASE OF MOTIVATION
    IN A NEW FACILITY   179
    The Approach at Shell Canada   179
    How Management and Union Leaders
       Felt about the Team Approach   181
    Labor-Management Cooperation and
       Mutual Trust   182

    INDEX   185

EXHIBITS

EXHIBIT 1.   Questionnaire for Employees of
Company X (Parts I and II)   16

EXHIBIT 2.   Questionnaire for Employees of
Company X (Part III)   24

EXHIBIT 3.   Tally Sheet   33

EXHIBIT 4.   Questionnaire for Exit Interview   46

EXHIBIT 5.   Checklist for Measuring a Job's
Satisfaction Potential   75

EXHIBIT 6.   Job-Subordinate Worksheet Form   110

EXHIBIT 7.   Job-Subordinate Worksheet
Sample   113

EXHIBIT 8.   Hewlett-Packard's Plan for MBO
at the Clerical Level   139

PREFACE

Motivation is not a packaged program or system that you can pick off a shelf and install in your workplace like a new carburetor in a sputtering car. You will not automatically transform yourself into a Norman Vincent Peale–type motivator just by reading this book.

But here's what will happen. You'll find it much easier to put your finger on the "motivational pulse" of your workers. You'll learn how to speed up a sluggish employee work rate. You'll find a wide choice of proven prescriptions for alleviating productivity ailments and getting subordinates' motivational juices flowing. And you'll be able to draw on the revealing experiences of other managers in devising your own overall approach to a successful motivational management style.

As an aggressive manager expanding your personal skills in this vital area, you'll also:

• Improve your overall ability to manage human resources

- Increase your own—and your workers'—job satisfaction

- Improve the quality of work life throughout your department

- Increase productivity and morale

- Contribute in a visible way to the smooth-running operations of your entire organization

- Receive recognition from your peers as an outstanding motivating manager

That may sound like a tall order for a single book. But there is one secret ingredient to this success formula: *you.* The personal touch is the essence of all motivation and productivity enhancement. There is no single, standardized "right way," because what we're talking about here is a people issue. Forget the doomsday prophecies about the dramatic decline in American worker productivity. Forget the academic pontificating on theories named after letters, not people. Forget the technological advances that transform mortals into mere robots.

Above all, remember that motivation and productivity involve people. You are people. Your workers are people. Your bosses (although you may sometimes have your doubts) are people, too.

The bottom line is this: How do you motivate people to increase their productivity? That is the basic question addressed in the three-step approach outlined in this book.

In Part I, you'll review a straightforward system for surveying the contours of your problem. Based on actual surveys and documented results, these chapters are light on theory and heavy on reality: preparing an employee questionnaire, conducting the study, calculating indices of the answers, analyzing the data, interpreting the results, creating a series of solutions.

You'll gain a realistic perspective on each aspect of this program through comprehensive reported findings. The results and recommendations from a real firm provide the thread that ties all the steps together. There's even a potpourri of findings from other actual studies to guide you in designing your own solutions.

In Part II, you'll find the implementation tools to solve any of the problems you uncover, techniques and methods that work in today's highly charged workplace. And you'll learn how to adopt a method of motivation management that will work for you.

Like a menu at a fine restaurant, the chapters in Part II offer a wide selection of options for you to choose from. They cover all the vital aspects of motivation, including feedback, teamwork, communications, recognition, job satisfaction, participation, goal setting, and more.

Finally in Part III, you can learn from the experiences of managers like yourself on the firing line of motivation and productivity in practice. Their ideas and suggestions will show you where they succeeded, and failed, in their efforts.

These case studies present you with the actual nuts and bolts on everything from the HP Way (Hewlett-Packard) to MBWA (Management by Wandering Around) to quality circles to the Involvement Corps (Occidental Insurance) to work teams.

What you'll eventually have is fuel for productive motivation management that needs only your imprint to help you move at an even faster pace on the road to a successful management career.

PART I

The first priority for an organized manager is to prepare a game plan. This is true whether you're trying to bolster an old argument or win approval for a new project, whether you're preparing a companywide presentation or sitting down in your office for a personal conference.

The key ingredient is preparation through research. The same principle applies to creating a management style that will motivate your people to greater productivity. And there's no better place to learn how to motivate a worker than from the individual worker.

That's why Part I of this book concentrates on surveys of your workers. Their results will help you see what the problems are, measure their impact, and find their solutions. A soundly constructed and intelligently conducted worker survey will suggest new ideas and methods that can generate measurable productivity improvements. The survey will also show your workers that you are indeed interested in what they think, and this will give morale a real shot in the arm.

The proper use of a good survey can also stamp you as a leader and innovator in the area of motivation management.

Taken by itself, a survey may be just a compilation of numbers and other data. But you can add the components that will make it come to life by following the outline in these first chapters. You ask the right questions, prepare a cogent analysis of the results, and suggest shrewd strategies to attack the problems that you uncover. In sum, you lay the foundation for your entire motivation program to improve productivity.

Your current method of research for motivation purposes may involve simply asking an individual what's wrong. And that method may be quite effective. For now. What happens, though, as your responsibilities expand? As you are placed in charge of larger numbers of employees? As supervisors and other managers come under your supervision? As entire departments or divisions are placed in your hands? Simply questioning individuals might not be enough after these changes occur. Now is the time to arm yourself for that future position. And this is the book to provide you with the shells.

PREPARING
A SYSTEM TO INCREASE
WORKER PRODUCTIVITY

All managers are increasingly concerned with the critical need for increased employee productivity. Continuing inflation intensifies the need for economy within the individual company and, coupled with pressures from competition, the need to get greater output from human resources. The problem of productivity in many companies has reached a point at which neither the injection of greater capital nor the application of traditional efficiency techniques can move it substantially above its present plateau.

A major cause of the productivity problem lies in the radical changes in attitudes, job satisfaction, and morale among workers. As management philosopher Peter Drucker noted in *Management: Tasks, Responsibilities, Practices*, "We do know that work and the work force are undergoing greater changes today than at any time since the beginning of the industrial revolution two centuries ago." These changes are having a negative effect on productivity.

The first step in learning how to cope with these changes

and increase productivity is to find out what is on the workers' minds. If you can uncover workers' opinions of their supervisors, their working conditions, and their jobs, then you can take actions that will improve productivity. At the very least, learning what is on employees' minds will help you head off problems before they lead to lateness, absenteeism, strikes, and personnel turnover.

This section focuses on a time-tested method of uncovering employee attitudes and opinions, developing morale indices, and giving the manager a basis on which to decide how to improve employee productivity. That method is the questionnaire.

There is no single, simple way to improve productivity, of course. The most popula: movement today is toward using job satisfaction to get this result. It is management's responsibility and the supervisors' task to see that employees are satisfied with their jobs.

Job satisfaction depends on many things, including working conditions, type of work, design of work, workers' attitudes toward the supervisor, their attitudes toward the company, and their personal problems. As with productivity, there is no single, simple answer to improving job satisfaction. But companies can take a first step to zero in on those aspects of job satisfaction that need improvement. This first step, the employee questionnaire, determines what is on workers' minds, measures employee morale, and pinpoints the needs that require satisfaction.

WHAT IS THE LINK
BETWEEN MORALE AND
PRODUCTIVITY?

On the effects of morale on productivity, Douglas Hall of Boston University said, "There is some evidence that productivity can be one [component of] job satisfaction. The more productive worker gets a sense of achievement and fulfillment that leads to satisfaction." Professor Hall believes that workers who become strongly involved in their jobs will be more productive. In brief, there are connections between job satisfaction and productivity.

Lewis Benton, a professor of management who is currently teaching in China after many years at Hofstra University, has spoken and written extensively about the relationship between morale and productivity. He said,

> Most people believe that high morale will always lead to high productivity. While this is not always true, in twenty studies of the link between the two, most of them show that high morale *is* associated with high productivity.
>
> The best interests of management are served if there is a constant awareness of the spirit and harmony of workers. That includes knowing employee attitudes toward the job, job satisfactions, and personal adjustment. If you keep continually aware of attitudes, you can take steps that should result in improved productivity. Management is finding it useful to try to anticipate and prevent problems from arising. In that connection, morale surveys are a valuable tool."

Dr. Benton's book, *Supervision and Management* (New York: McGraw-Hill, 1972), provides many ways to eliminate unrest and dissatisfaction that may cause poor morale among workers.

WHAT COMPANIES ARE DOING

Because of the links between morale, job satisfaction, and productivity, many companies survey employees on a regular basis. Attitude surveys, morale surveys, opinion surveys all have two common purposes: to give employees a chance to let management know their feelings about their employment, and to give management a chance to make adjustments that will result in better working conditions.

Thomas Comeaux directs Sears Organizational Surveys, a unit of Sears Roebuck and Co., which attempts to survey all hourly employees regularly so that each person will be surveyed every three years.

The survey of hourly employees attempts to measure employee attitudes on eight subjects:

1. supervision

2. kind of work

3. amount of work

4. pay and benefits

5. physical surroundings

6. co-workers

7. career future and job security

8. company identification

Top management feels strongly that there is a definite link between employee morale and productivity. Management's commitment to this belief is shown by the massive size of the undertaking.

Sears views this survey as a management tool. As the results of the opinions of employees are determined, management takes appropriate steps to improve any negative condition that is revealed.

ANOTHER VIEW OF MORALE SURVEYS

According to John Hinrichs, who for thirteen years was involved in supervising personnel research and management development activities for International Business Machines in the United States and abroad, IBM measured morale regularly by survey. Each person was surveyed once a year. Because of IBM's size, the worldwide surveys were done in cycles. In this way top management got a sample of employee opinions every six months.

The questions asked covered people's feelings about pay, supervision, demands of the job, physical working conditions, and the like. Regarding the link between morale and productivity, Dr. Hinrichs said that IBM found a strong link between morale, turnover of personnel, and absenteeism. IBM was able to predict the rate of turnover of personnel six months in advance as a result of its use of regular surveys.

Now president of Management Decisions Systems, Inc., a broad-based research publishing and consulting firm dealing with problems of human resource management, Dr. Hinrichs says, "The survey process provides well-managed firms with unique inputs for assessing the motivational impact of management decisions as well as a continuing discipline for opening communications and solving problems."

One thing seems quite clear: people need a chance to express themselves on the subject of their employment, and management needs to know what these employees' feelings are. If management takes appropriate steps after the data are gathered, measuring morale regularly is a positive step forward in identifying existing problems as well as the components that make up job satisfaction.

ATTITUDES, JOB SATISFACTION, AND EMPLOYEE MORALE

Morale is an emotional attribute. It provides energy, acceptance of leadership, and cooperation among members of a group. Because the word is used with so many different meanings, or used synonymously with "attitudes" and "job satisfaction," here are definitions of the words as used in this book:

- *An attitude* is an individual employee's feeling (satisfaction, indifference, or dissatisfaction) toward a specific subject, situation, object, or person. Attitudes are formed about *subjects*, such as religion, politics, life insurance, production scheduling, accident prevention, company policies; about *situations*, such as falling company profits, merging with a larger company, construction of a competitive plant, discontinuance of a product, introduction of new machinery; about *objects*, such as equipment, tools, workplaces, lighting, materials; and about *persons*, such as the foreman, plant manager, fellow employees, spouse, and government inspectors. Many things influence employee attitudes: home, education, mores of social groups, attitudes of fellow employees, kinds of supervision, physical environment of workplaces, adaptation to tasks, and expectations.

  Because management cannot control all these influences, it can never expect to satisfy all employees all the time. However, the planning based on data gleaned from a morale survey can remove irritants, introduce improvements, open more communication channels, and provide recognition. It can also help establish a climate of confidence in which employees can perform their tasks better and can derive greater job satisfaction.

- *Job satisfaction* is the net result of various attitudes held by an individual employee at a given period of time. It is subject to swings from one extreme to the other, but usually reverts to a fairly stable level that can be good or poor.

- *Employee morale* is the net result of the job satisfactions of the employees in a specified group, such as a department, a night shift, employees over fifty years of age, all female employees, or other groups.

This book takes the view that individual employees have attitudes and composite job satisfactions, but only groups of employees can reveal morale.

WAYS TO STUDY
EMPLOYEE MORALE

At least three methods have been devised to study employee morale:

1. Analyzing company records for changes in resignations, lateness, absenteeism, productivity, and complaints. This is an inefficient method, since it measures effects and not causes.

2. Interviewing employees, using prepared questions or simply allowing employees to talk about anything they desire. This method is costly and time-consuming.

3. Administering unsigned questionnaires to groups of employees. Results are expressed either as percentages or as morale indices. We will focus on this third method. The questionnaire described later measures morale at a given period of time.

Percentages and morale indices can be compared with those compiled from previous surveys, or they can be tabulated to compare one department with another. Surveys should be conducted periodically, not just once. As the Sears and IBM examples indicate, some organizations conduct surveys as frequently as twice a year; most settle for administering them annually.

Many managers have no standards by which to evaluate the results of their first survey. You can overcome that obstacle by using scores from consulting firms that specialize in conducting such surveys. They have compiled data from a number of frequently asked questions, and they have developed scores from actual surveys they conducted. These may suffice for comparison purposes until you have a data base of your own. When you make your second and subsequent surveys, you can compare the percentages and indices to them. Comparisons of a series of scores over time will reveal trends that will help you determine whether your attempts to improve morale and productivity are succeeding.

2

DETERMINING MORALE THROUGH THE UNSIGNED QUESTIONNAIRE

Exhibit 1 shows an actual survey questionnaire that Benge Associates used at a company that manufactures electronic components (Company X). Throughout the next few chapters, this questionnaire will serve as a model.

The first page of the questionnaire explains its purpose to the respondees. It is intended to solicit from them honest answers by inspiring in them trust that the results of the survey will be kept completely anonymous. This trust must never be violated.

Part I elicits employees' age, earnings, tenure, and department. When a department has only one or two employees, they may feel reluctant to reveal their work stations for fear of identifying themselves. In this situation, you should list joint departments such as "Inspection, Shipping, and Receiving." Supervisors should not be required to specify their departments if doing so will endanger their anonymity. Many companies also ask the respondents' sex and what shift they work. These additions provide a fifth and sixth category for tabulation.

The rest of the questionnaire is designed to determine the attitudes and morale of the workers. The first nineteen questions in Part II are intended to supply data to use in calculating morale indices.

ASKING THE RIGHT KINDS OF QUESTIONS

Questions can be asked in various ways. Here are sample questions, with comments on their use.

1. Write below how you think the lighting at your place of work could be improved:

   This is an open-ended question. Part III of the questionnaire (Exhibit 2) gives additional open-ended questions. Normally on the first survey, about 10 percent of the respondents answer these questions with comments or complaints. These yield valuable information, the treatment of which is discussed later. However, such open-ended questions cannot be used for numerical analysis.

2. Is lighting at your workplace satisfactory?

   Yes _____

   No _____

   This type of question allows only a positive or negative response and is of limited value in determining morale.

3. Which *one* of the following should be stressed in the employee newspaper:

   Pictures of employees   _____

Company plans for the future   _____

News of families, weddings,
etc.   _____

Messages from the president   _____

Employee athletic events   _____

Jokes and cartoons   _____

Questions like this are useful in calculating percentage responses.

4. Is lighting at your workplace:

Very poor   _____

Not good enough   _____

Sufficient   _____

Very good   _____

Excellent   _____

This multiple-choice question is easy to quantify. When responses could cover a range from low to high, it's best to use the multiple-choice form.

Only multiple choice questions like type 4 can be used to compute a morale index. Types 2 and 3 can be used to calculate percentages, however.

You may want to use some questions in the sample survey or none at all. When your draft of the survey is finished, you can pass copies to colleagues and trusted subordinates and elicit valuable suggestions. Use your own ingenuity and creativity to adapt either this survey or another to your own requirements. The more thought you give to devising the questions the more helpful your employees' answers will be.

EXHIBIT 1

Questionnaire for Employees of Company X (Parts I and II)

In an attempt to make Company X a better place to work, your company has requested that we make this attitude survey.

This questionnaire gives you an opportunity to state clearly how you feel about your job. You can be perfectly frank about your responses, for you are not to sign your name, nor will this questionnaire ever be shown to your employers or to anyone representing them. It is an honest endeavor on the part of management to find out what employees really think, so that management policies and employee relationships can be strengthened.

When you have filled out this questionnaire, place it in the locked box. The questionnaires will be removed to the offices of Benge Associates for analysis and tabulation. A report will be made to your company summarizing employees' viewpoints, but the questionnaires themselves will not be shown to management. This study is important for your future work happiness. Be honest . . . be fair in your replies.

Benge Associates
Management Consultants

This questionnaire is divided into three parts. Part I asks for general information: your age, hourly earnings, length of service, and department. Part II asks you to indicate your reaction to a number of present practices and policies. Note that you merely mark your answer with an X. No other writing is necessary. However, space is provided in Part III on the final page for you to write any additional remarks, if you so desire.

Don't forget: be frank and be fair. Now start with No. 1 below and complete the questions in order please. Take your time, and don't confer with any fellow employees as to how you should answer any question. Give your own honest opinions.

PART I

Place a cross (X) beside the statements that apply to you personally:

1. IN AGE I AM:
( ) A. 24 or under
( ) B. Between 25 and 29
( ) C. Between 30 and 39
( ) D. 40 or over

2. MY HOURLY EARNINGS ARE FROM:
( ) A. $ per hr. - per hr.
( ) B. $ per hr. - per hr.
( ) C. $ per hr. - per hr.
( ) D. $ per hr. - per hr.

3. I HAVE WORKED FOR THE COMPANY
   APPROXIMATELY:
( ) A. Under 1 year
( ) B. 1 to 4 years
( ) C. 5 to 9 years
( ) D. 10 years or over

4. DURING THE LAST MONTH I HAVE
   WORKED ENTIRELY OR MAINLY IN
   THE FOLLOWING DEPARTMENT:
   (MARK ONE ONLY)
( ) A. Assembly—manual
( ) B. Assembly—machine
( ) C. Maintenance
( ) D. Plating
( ) E. Punch Press
( ) F. Tool Room
( ) G. Molding
( ) H. Deflashing
( ) I. Shipping and Receiving
( ) J. Distributor
( ) K. Inspection

PART II

To indicate your answer to each question, merely place an X in the space before the statement that most nearly expresses your opinion.

YOUR JOB

1. How do you like your present job?
( ) A. I don't like it
( ) B. I'd prefer something else
( ) C. I just accept it, neither liking nor disliking it
( ) D. All things considered, I like it pretty well
( ) E. I like it fine

2. Is the atmosphere of your workplace:
( ) A. Extremely hot, cold, draughty, or dusty
( ) B. Usually unpleasant
( ) C. Occasionally unpleasant
( ) D. Generally satisfactory
( ) E. Excellent most of the time

3. Is the lighting at your workplace:
( ) A. Very bad
( ) B. Poor
( ) C. Just barely good enough
( ) D. All right
( ) E. Just right for the work to be done

4. How about your ability to do your job?
( ) A. I have a lot more ability than my job calls for
( ) B. My job doesn't make use of many things I can do well
( ) C. My job makes use of some things I can do well
( ) D. My job just about fits me
( ) E. I think I am where I now belong and that my present job will lead to a better one

5. For the most part, fellow employees in my department are:

( ) A. Unfriendly   ( ) D. Cooperative
( ) B. Indifferent to me   ( ) E. Very friendly
( ) C. All right

6. Compared to other pay rates in your office or plant, do you consider your rate:

( ) A. Extremely low   ( ) D. Above average
( ) B. On the low side   ( ) E. Quite generous
( ) C. About right

7. How about the chances of your getting hurt on the job?

( ) A. There are lots of chances of getting hurt; some could be eliminated
( ) B. There are still plenty of chances of getting hurt, although the company has eliminated some of them
( ) C. There is some chance of getting hurt, but it is not bad
( ) D. Most chances of getting hurt have been eliminated
( ) E. There is not much chance of getting hurt on my job

THE BOSS
The next 7 questions refer to your manager or immediate supervisor.

8. In attitude toward you personally, is your boss:

( ) A. Always unfair
( ) B. Often unfair
( ) C. Sometimes fair, sometimes unfair
( ) D. Usually fair
( ) E. Fair at all times

9.   If you have a complaint, how does your boss usually receive it?
( )   A.   Does nothing about it
( )   B.   Usually tries to talk me out of it
( )   C.   Passes it on to a higher boss, but generally nothing happens
( )   D.   Listens carefully and acts on those that seem just
( )   E.   Accepts all complaints in good spirit and investigates, then gives a clear decision

10.   How well does your manager or supervisor keep you informed on company policy, plans, and developments?
( )   A.   Not at all
( )   B.   Seems not too well informed
( )   C.   Informs me some of the time
( )   D.   Most of the time
( )   E.   All of the time

11.   How well does your supervisor plan the work of your group:
( )   A.   There is no planning
( )   B.   Occasional planning, but not good
( )   C.   Tries to plan most of it
( )   D.   Work is regularly planned
( )   E.   Careful, systematic planning at all times

12.   How well does the supervisor explain new things to employees:
( )   A.   Never bothers
( )   B.   Explanations are not clear
( )   C.   Sometimes explains quite well
( )   D.   Most of the time gives clear instructions
( )   E.   Explains carefully and patiently

13.   How does your supervisor discipline employees who deserve it?
( )   A.   Bawls them out in front of other employees
( )   B.   Uses sarcasm in front of other employees

( ) C. Is quite direct, but takes employees aside
( ) D. Criticizes in private and explains why
( ) E. Criticicisms are always helpful and never given
         in the presence of others

14. I believe that my boss:
( ) A. Is not qualified for the job
( ) B. Lacks some necessary qualifications
( ) C. Is fairly well qualified
( ) D. Is quite well qualified
( ) E. Is highly qualified

YOUR COMPANY
15. Compared with other employers in your community,
     how well does this company treat its employees?
( ) A. Most others are better
( ) B. A few others are better
( ) C. About as well as the average
( ) D. Our company is better than most
( ) E. Ours is decidedly the best

16. Do you feel that the company:
( ) A. Has little genuine regard for employees
( ) B. Looks upon them as workers rather than as
         human beings
( ) C. Gets by satisfactorily in handling employees
( ) D. Really understands employee problems
( ) E. Shows high regard for the employees' welfare

17. In its relationships with the community, I believe our
     company:
( ) A. Has built ill will
( ) B. Does not have the respect of the citizens
( ) C. Should do more than it has
( ) D. Has built some good will
( ) E. Has built a lot of good will

18. When you tell your friends what company you work
     for, how do you feel?

( ) A. Ashamed to admit it
( ) B. Not happy about it
( ) C. Neutral about it
( ) D. Glad I don't work for certain other companies
( ) E. Proud to tell it

19. In its relations between employees and management, I think the company is:
( ) A. Doing a poor job
( ) B. Has considerable room for improvement
( ) C. About average
( ) D. Pretty good
( ) E. Decidedly outstanding

20. Which one of the following in your opinion shows greatest consideration to employees:
( ) A. Your immediate supervisor
( ) B. Manager of the department
( ) C. Top management of the company

21. Which one of the following in your opinion shows the least consideration to employees:
( ) A. Your immediate supervisor
( ) B. Manager of the department
( ) C. Top management of the company

22. The care and maintenance given to washrooms and toilets is:
( ) A. Poor
( ) B. Fair
( ) C. Good

23. The cleanliness of the lunch room is:
( ) A. Poor
( ) B. Fair
( ) C. Good

24. The food and vending machines are:
( ) A. Poor
( ) B. Okay
( ) C. Quite satisfactory

25. Prices in the cafeteria are:
( ) A. Entirely too high
( ) B. Okay
( ) C. Quite reasonable

26. What percentages of profit on sales after paying taxes do you think your company makes?
( ) A. 1 percent
( ) B. 5 percent
( ) C. 10 percent
( ) D. 15 percent
( ) E. 20 percent or more

27. What is your opinion of your company's method of inducting and training new employees?
( ) A. Not enough attention is given to new employees
( ) B. I have no opinion on this matter
( ) C. They are being well treated and properly trained

28. How much do you think the company has to pay for hospitalization insurance for each employee annually?
( ) A. $50.00–$100.00
( ) B. $105.00– $150.00
( ) C. $155.00–$200.00
( ) D. $205.00–$250.00
( ) E. $255.00 or more

29. Do you feel that prompt action is taken on safety recommendations?
( ) A. No
( ) B. Sometimes
( ) C. Yes

30.   Do you frequently receive orders from more than one
      person?
( ) A. No
( ) B. Yes

31.   If you answered yes above, do orders sometimes
      conflict?
( ) A. No
( ) B. Yes

32.   How do you feel about working overtime:
( ) A. Do not like it at all
( ) B. Do not mind it occasionally
( ) C. Neutral about it
( ) D. Like it all the time

EXHIBIT 2

Questionnaire for Employees of Company X (Part III)

Part III

    If you wish to offer any suggestions or criticisms not cov-
ered by your answeres in Parts I and II, you may use the space
below. Your comments will be typed and included in the report
made to your company showing the results of these questionnaires—but these forms will never be seen by any supervisor
or executive of your company. So, if you wish, write anything
you want to. You are not required to write anything here unless
you want to. *Do not sign your name.*

Additional comments about your *JOB*:

Additional comments about your immediate *SUPERVISOR*:

Additional comments about your *COMPANY*:

Any other comments:

When you have completed your guestionnaire, fold it once and drop into the locked box. Thanks for your cooperation.

BENGE ASSOCIATES

3

TECHNIQUES
FOR ADMINISTERING
THE QUESTIONNAIRE

Having planned the survey and developed the questionnaire, you must find an impartial administrator from outside the company to administer the questionnaire to employee groups. A respected educator, consultant, secretary of an employers' association, or a well-known civic leader can provide this service. The personnel manager or other company managers should *not* administer the survey. If they do, suspicious employees may not answer truthfully or may withhold pertinent information.

Questionnaires should be distributed to employees in a group meeting. Workers should not be allowed to take them home to fill out. If they do that, the results will be influenced by other people. Moreover, experience shows that fewer than half of the questionnaires will be returned when employees are allowed to fill out the questionnaire on their own time, off the company's premises. The best results are obtained by gathering employees in groups, the number depending on the seating capacity of the available room.

When the company cannot make a meeting room available, the outside administrator can go from one department to the next, explaining the survey and distributing questionnaires. Then the employees can complete the questionnaires at their workplace and place them in a locked box provided for this purpose.

EXPLAINING THE QUESTIONNAIRE

Here's a typical presentation to an employee group:

My name is Lee Smith. As some of you know, I am a consultant and am not employed by this company. Because I am impartial, your management has asked me to conduct this entire survey.

The form that I will hand out contains questions about your thoughts on your job, your working conditions, your supervisor, and your company's practices. All questions can be answered with an X or a check mark; you don't have to write anything. However, if you want to offer suggestions or make complaints, you can do so on the fourth page. Do *not* sign the questionnaire.

When you have finished, fold the survey form just once, and drop it into the locked box at the exit. You can be quite frank in your answers, for no one in your company will ever see your questionnaire. I will open the box, tabulate the answers, calculate percentages, report the data to management, and destroy the forms.

If you write anything on the fourth page, I'll have your comment typed and submit it to management. Its source will not be revealed.

This is not an examination. There is no time limit. If you have any questions or need help, raise your hand and I'll try to assist you.

The administrator should give each employee group an hour to complete the questionnaire. Fast readers will finish a four-page questionnaire in twenty minutes. As employees finish, they should deposit their questionnaires in a box, preferably locked to reinforce further the administrator's promise of confidentiality.

Some employees may be unsure as to which of the listed departments they belong; they may know only the names of their sections. The administrator should have a list of all sections of the listed departments. If no list is available, experienced fellow employees can usually identify the employee's department.

Foremen and other supervisors should not be in the same group with their subordinates. Also, to preserve their anonymity, they should not check their departments on the survey form.

EDITING QUESTIONNAIRES

Many employees, especially those who are poorly educated, will make errors. The most common are:

- Marking two responses to a single question. When this happens, the administrator accepts the response of greater numerical value.

- Marking two departments. If questionnaires have been administered to departmental groups, the administrator estimates the correct department and crosses the other out.

- Writing in responses other than those printed. These can be ignored or regarded as comments elicited in Part III.

- Omitting answers. Omissions must be tallied.

- Signing the questionnaire. The administrator ignores the signature and does not record or report it.

The administrator should number and edit each survey form to facilitate tabulation.

ADMINISTERING THE QUESTIONNAIRE IN DECENTRALIZED COMPANIES

Some decentralized companies have many locations, making it difficult or costly for one person to administer the survey to all employees. In this situation, questionnaires are sent to each location along with stamped envelopes to be mailed to the administrator's business address. An accompanying letter to location managers directs them to explain the study to their employees, distribute the questionnaires, and have the employees mail the completed forms to the administrator. Unfortunately, experience shows that not all employees will return their questionnaires.

MORALE INDICES:
HOW TO CALCULATE AND
INTERPRET THEM

You may now be convinced that a morale survey is just the right method to determine the attitude of your employees, discover more productive work methods, and enhance your stature in upper management's eyes. But you can really earn your spurs in the planning and preparation that you put into the survey. It is not enough to establish your goals and develop the questions you want answered. The other steps you must take are explained in this chapter.

PLANNING THE FORMAT

One of the most important—and most often overlooked—aspects of a morale survey is the format. If you don't have a detailed and carefully constructed method of tabulating the questionnaire, you'll spend an inordinate amount of time calculating the answers. You'll also have trouble interpreting the results. You can make the answers easy to tabulate and analyze by using indices. That's what these next two chapters will cover.

One word of warning. There is a big difference in how you approach large surveys as opposed to smaller ones. If you have many questions (say over twenty-five), a lot of employee categories you want to cover (more than a half-dozen), and a great many employees you want to survey (over two hundred), you'll probably want to use a computer and/or hire a research consultant.

The widespread use of the small computer has made these large surveys much easier to accomplish. But you don't need one. Some of the most successful and productive employee surveys today are developed and tabulated by hand. Those are the kind you'll find explained here. The questionnaire from Chapter 2 will serve as the basis, so you'll have a firm foundation in how indices are developed and numbers manipulated to create a final analysis.

SETTING UP THE TABULATION

Exhibit 3 shows a partial tally sheet for hand tabulating. You'll need a master tally sheet of this kind for each category of employee that you want to measure or compare.

Suppose you want to measure the morale in your purchasing department only. Simple. Use one tally sheet with a segment allocated to each question.

More likely you'll want to assess several categories of employees. The questionnaire in Exhibit 1 covers twenty-three different categories in four general areas in the first four questions: age, earnings, tenure, and department.

If you want to cross-tabulate among these categories, a computer will definitely come in handy. For example, suppose you want to compare the attitudes of molding department employees over forty making $12.50 an hour who have been with the company five to nine years with maintenance department employees under twenty-four making $6.50 an hour who have been with the company one to four years. It would take you an eternity to sort out the employees who fit those categories if you do the job by hand. A computer, coded correctly, could do it in the blink of an eye.

A more standard approach would be to separate into categories according to the general area. That way, you'd make four piles of questionnaires for Question 1 in Part I. Each pile would represent a specific age group, checked by A, B, C, or D. Then you could compare attitudes by age. The same would be true of Questions 2 and 3 in Part I. However, Question 4 would have eleven piles of questionnaires for A through K.

But suppose you just want to compare two departments to see why productivity is higher in one than it is in the other. Or you want to analyze the attitude differences between young and old employees. This job is easy to do by hand, and the results will be just as valuable.

The Tally Process in Action

Exhibit 3 reflects the results of the survey of employees in the molding department. It is just the beginning of the tabulation, covering Questions 1, 2, 3, and part of 4 from Part II.

Forty employees were surveyed in this department. A clerk tabulated the answers with a short stroke opposite the option checked for each question—either A, B, C, D, or E. (You'll soon see why there are five choices for each question.) If no answer is checked, the stroke goes next to the X under the Total line. You can see that three people didn't answer Question 1; one didn't answer Question 2.

EXHIBIT 3

Tally Sheet

Number of questionnaires: 40   **Group** Molding Dept.

Item	Tally	%	No.	Extension	Index
1 A	|||	8	3	6	
B	ℍℍ		16	6	24	
C	ℍℍ ||||	24	9	54	
D	ℍℍ ℍℍ |||	36	13	104	
E	ℍℍ		16	6	60	
Totals		100	37	248	67
X					
			3		
2 A			3	1	2	
B	ℍℍ		13	5	20	
C	ℍℍ		15	6	36	
D	ℍℍ ℍℍ ℍℍ		41	16	128	
E	ℍℍ ℍℍ		28	11	110	
Totals		100	39	296	76
X					
			1		

3 A 〽️ │	15	6	12	
B 〽️ 〽️ ││	30	12	48	
C 〽️ 〽️ ││││	35	14	84	
D 〽️ │	15	6	48	
E ││	5	2	20	
Totals_____	100	40	212	53
X				
4 A │││	8	3	6	
B 〽️ │	15	16	64	
C 〽️ ││││	22	9	54	

There are four columns on the right side of Exhibit 3. The first is the Percentage column, and the second is the Number column. Three employees, or 8 percent of the workers in this department checked letter A in the first question; six, or 16 percent, checked B; and so on.

Take a look at Question 1: How do you like your present job? You find the raw data tell you that:

- Three employees, or 8 percent, do not like their jobs.

- Six, or 16 percent, would prefer something else.

- Nine, or 24 percent, just accept their jobs.

- Thirteen, or 36 percent, like their jobs pretty well.

- Six, or 16 percent, like their jobs a lot.

While these raw data do give you a certain amount of insight, they are difficult to use effectively, especially in comparisons and cross-tabulations. You can be overwhelmed by the mass of numbers. To put the information into a simpler and more understandable form and make your interpretation that much more valuable, you should utilize a morale index.

COMPILING A MORALE INDEX

The morale index is a weighted composite of five percentages. It can be calculated either arithmetically or in percentages. The Extension column in Exhibit 3 shows the index method obtained arithmetically.

The morale index can be used only if there are five possible choices ranging from a very negative attitude to a very positive attitude. It cannot be calculated on two, three, four, or more than five responses. For such questions, percentages are used. You multiply the figures in the Number column according to this formula:

- The figure in the Number column opposite the first response (A) is multiplied by 2.

- The figure in the Number column opposite the second response (B) is multiplied by 4.

- The figure in the Number column opposite the third response (C) is multiplied by 6.

- The figure in the Number column opposite the fourth response (D) is multiplied by 8.

- The figure in the Number column opposite the fifth response (E) is multiplied by 10.

After you multiply and put the totals in the appropriate space in the Extension column, you add those totals. You can see in Exhibit 3 that the total Extension number for Question 1 is 248; the total for Question 2 is 296.

Next, you add the numbers in the Number column for each question. The total for Question 1 is 37; for Question 2 the total is 39. Then divide the total in the Extension column (248 for Question 1) by the total in the Number column (37). The result is 6.7. To turn that number into a morale index simply multiply it by 10. The result here is a morale index for the molding department's response to the question, "How do you like your job?"

The morale index is 67. If you performed the same calculations for the maintenance department's responses, you could compare the morale of the two departments. And if you noted the molding department's index today and gave the same questionnaire six months later after incorporating some morale boosters into the department, you could compare the two indices and see if those new morale boosters worked.

Calculating Morale Indices in Percentages

You can use a percentage method to obtain the same results. Use the same series of multipliers: 2, 4, 6, 8, 10. For the first question, you'd get a formula like this:

- 8 percent multiplied by 2 equals an extension of 16

- 16 percent multiplied by 4 equals an extension of 64

- 24 percent multiplied by 6 equals an extension of 144

- 36 percent multiplied by 8 equals an extension of 288

- 16 percent multiplied by 10 equals an extension of 160

Add the Extension totals, and you get 672. Divide that number by 10. The result (67) matches the finding when you used the arithmetic method.

USING MORALE INDICES

The value of morale indices becomes clear when you interpret their results. By itself, the morale index of job satisfaction of 67 in the molding department means little; it's just a number.

But suppose you had the same index for maintenance, purchasing, and other departments. You could compare any two or three, or all the departments. You'd see where morale was high, low, and medium. If you conducted similar surveys at specific intervals in the future, you could see whether certain programs had worked, where morale was slipping or improving, and where to focus revitalization efforts.

Here are some standard categories you can compare based on the first four questions in Exhibit 1.

Category	Subdivisions
Age	Young vs. average vs. old
Earnings	Low vs. average vs. high
Length of service	Short vs. average vs. long
Departments	Any two or more

Tailor your categories to your needs. Perhaps you'd like to do a comparison of male versus female employees, or day shift versus night shift personnel.

Another way to use these indices is in a composite manner. To do this, you prepare the questions in your survey by broad area. You can see in Exhibit 1 that the general areas are Your Job, The Boss, and Your Company. By calculating the morale index for each question in a specific area, adding them together, and dividing by the number of questions, you get a composite picture of employee attitudes in that sector. You can then compare the overall attitude of the employees in the molding department toward their jobs with that of the employees in maintenance toward their jobs, or the attitude of new workers toward management (The Boss) with that of older workers.

You'll see more on this analysis method in the next chapter. But this gives you a good idea of how valuable a morale index is as a comparison calculation that can spur action plans to increase morale and productivity.

5

ANALYZING DATA
FROM MORALE INDICES

You can use the results obtained from your morale indices in a number of analyses. You can compare attitudes by department, among wage earners, for the whole company, from one period to the next, and so forth.

You cannot use them, however, to compare individual questions against each other by using their index numbers. For example, suppose the question on lighting in the workplace (Question 3, Exhibit 1) elicits a higher morale index number than the one on atmosphere in the workplace (Question 2, Exhibit 1). That does not mean that you can say with complete assurance that employees were more satisfied with the lighting than they were with the atmosphere. Likewise, it would not be fruitful to compare the question on lighting with that on friendliness of fellow employees (Question 5, Exhibit 1). That would be like comparing apples and oranges.

ANALYZING PERCENTAGE FINDINGS

Certain questions do not lend themselves to indices, and should instead be analyzed in terms of percentages. Such questions are exemplified by Questions 20–32 in Exhibit 1. You'll notice that they don't have the requisite five degrees of attitude; some have three options, some have four, and some five. For example, Question 20 asks about employee perception of management consideration. Let's suppose that the percentages for that item were as follows:

20. Which one of the following in your opinion shows greatest consideration to employees?

A.	Your immediate superior	52 percent
B.	Manager of the department	6 percent
C.	Top management of the company	42 percent

In this instance, you value each percentage on its own merits. You could interpret these results as meaning this particular department manager is very unpopular—or very unknown. Here is where a continuing survey program is valuable. Suppose you instituted a deliberate program to have this department manager assume a higher profile and become more considerate in dealing with employees. After six months, you could conduct this portion of the survey again and find out whether the program is working or whether you still have a problem.

COMPARING DEPARTMENTS

The comparison of departmental morale figures is the most useful analysis. Other categories (age, sex, shift, earnings, and length of service) give companywide information, but departmental data pinpoint department morale levels, job satisfaction, and productivity problems. In companies employing thousands of workers, departmental figures can be broken down according to other categories such as shift, age, and so forth. In small and medium-sized organizations, however, the tabulation comparing departments will prove adequate. Percentage comparisons (for Questions 20 to 32 in Exhibit 1, for example) will also be informative.

On the following page, there is a comparison of morale indices for four departments of Company X in Exhibit 1. Various conclusions can be drawn from this tabulation: employees in the manual assembly department like their jobs; maintenance department employees like their foreman, but are otherwise dissatisfied; plating department shows low morale throughout, and so on.

For discussion in management and supervisory groups, some companies prepare a series of charts. Such charts can also be prepared on color slides for more elaborate and striking presentations.

ANALYZING INITIAL SURVEYS

If you're planning to conduct your first survey and use some of the questions from Exhibit 1, you can use these figures on page 43 for comparison. These nineteen questions are standard and have been asked in survey after survey. You can compare your results with those listed here with assurance that your analysis will be accurate. Or you can use these figures as benchmarks to shoot for in planning subsequent improvements.

A few words of advice. Utilities, service, and commercial organizations usually have higher figures. Small

Ques-tion	Subject	Assembly Manual	Assembly Machine	Mainte-nance	Plating
1	Like present job	82	76	73	70
2	Atmosphere	71	66	61	56
3	Lighting	70	65	60	63
4	Use of abilities	70	68	63	64
5	Fellow employees	88	82	76	77
6	Pay rates	52	44	40	42
7	Accident risk	68	62	58	62
	Average morale index for questions about job	**72**	**66**	**62**	**62**
8	Attitude of boss	74	73	77	74
9	Complaint handling	68	69	70	69
10	Informs employees	72	72	75	72
11	Plans work	66	64	68	62
12	Explains new things	71	73	76	74
13	Disciplines employ-ees	69	70	74	70
14	Qualified for the job	72	73	79	75
	Average morale index for questions about boss	**70**	**71**	**74**	**71**
15	Comparison with oth-er employers	66	65	62	64
16	Regard for employees	68	66	62	66
17	Community relations	68	66	62	66
18	Pride in company	69	65	63	67
19	Employee-manage-ment relations	64	62	60	63
	Average morale index for questions about company	**67**	**66**	**64**	**65**
	Average morale index for all 19 questions	**70**	**68**	**67**	**66**

Question	Subject of Question	Standard Average Morale Index
1	Like present job	79
2	Atmosphere	64
3	Lighting	64
4	Use of abilities	68
5	Fellow employees	80
6	Pay rates	44
7	Accident risk	67

Average morale index for questions about jobs **67**

8	Attitude of boss	78
9	Complaint handling	71
10	Informs employees	75
11	Plans work	65
12	Explains new things	75
13	Disciplines employees	75
14	Qualified for the job	73

Average morale index for questions about boss **73**

15	Comparison with other employers	66
16	Regard for employees	66
17	Community relations	79
18	Pride in company	67
19	Employee-management relations	70

Average morale index for questions about company **70**

Average morale index for all 19 questions **70**

variations from these figures are significant *for large groups*. Thus, if several hundred employees are included in a survey, a companywide accident-risk index of 65 against an average index of 67 shows that employees in this company are more fearful of accidents than normal. The difference would not be significant for a group of twelve employees, however.

No matter how big or small your company, though, be on the lookout for variations from the standard indices given here. Even if the variations are not definitive, they may point you in a new direction or enable you to combine two seemingly disparate trends into one insightful analysis.

COMPARISONS IN ACTION

Most companies are eager to compare the results of their first and second surveys. One company, an electric utility, was pleased to see general improvement across the board in most areas, but it was less sanguine about the fact that all areas did not show similar amounts of improvement.

Following the first survey, the management at that company had put much effort into planning a program to improve employee relations based on the survey findings. This program evolved from a discussion among its top ten managers. As usual, some managers agreed to the plans but did not follow through on the recommendations. When the results of the second survey were presented, there were red faces in abundance. Subsidiary charts showed exactly which managers had failed to implement the program. They were roundly chastised. Even upper-level heads rolled: a vice-president retired and was replaced with a more progressive and cooperative assistant.

Managers who had not been involved in the first survey

were clearly impressed, not only by the extensive action the company took as a result of the second survey but also by the important improvements that had occurred as a result of actions recommended after the first survey.

All of this drove home the point that implementation is just as important as fact gathering. In other words, you must do more than take surveys and tabulate results before you can sit back and pat yourself on the back.

The steps you take to implement change are vitally important, and this is where an ingenious manager can shine. Interpret the results of the survey carefully. Forcefully bring them to the attention of those who have the power to take action and set policy. Then take the vital step of motivating people to carry out newly established programs so that they produce the desired results. Manager motivation and employee motivation combined will hit the productivity jackpot. We will have more to say about motivation in Part II.

For now, concentrate on survey information. Discussions of top and middle management should be built around the valuable information contained in survey reports. Some companies hold regularly scheduled meetings over weeks and months to hammer home the lessons to be learned from the surveys.

Take the lead whenever you can in those meetings. Have plenty of suggestions to offer. Make sure you are recognized as a mover and shaker in this vital management function.

Another type of survey often provides just as much information about employee attitudes as the morale questionnaire does. That is the *exit interview*.

Exhibit 4 contains twenty-seven questions that could elicit valuable information from employees leaving your company. You can use this information to shape your eventual motivation program.

EXHIBIT 4

Questionnaire for Exit Interview

Circle the response that best describes your feelings using the following key:

1. Strongly agree
2. Agree
3. Neutral
4. Disagree
5. Strongly disagree

1.	The work I was doing, on the whole, was approximately what I originally expected to be doing.	1	2	3	4	5
2.	Compared to what I initially thought, my superiors demanded a lot less of me.	1	2	3	4	5
3.	I wanted more responsibility than the company gave me.	1	2	3	4	5
4.	The people I worked with were interesting and stimulating.	1	2	3	4	5
5.	Generally, my co-workers were friendly and supportive.	1	2	3	4	5
6.	Overall, I was satisfied with the general working conditions.	1	2	3	4	5
7.	I had the necessary freedom to make my own decisions.	1	2	3	4	5
8.	I would recommend the company to my friends as a good organization to work for.	1	2	3	4	5

9.	There was too much pressure on the job.	1	2	3	4	5
10.	I found my work load to be excessive.	1	2	3	4	5
11.	I found my work to be interesting and challenging.	1	2	3	4	5
12.	I was able to make good use of my skills and abilities.	1	2	3	4	5
13.	I had ample opportunities for personal training and career development.	1	2	3	4	5
14.	I had ample opportunities to advance within the company.	1	2	3	4	5
15.	I knew that if I performed well, I would get ahead.	1	2	3	4	5
16.	The company's performance appraisal system accurately reflected my strengths and weaknesses.	1	2	3	4	5
17.	In my division/department, salary increases and promotions are clearly linked with performance.	1	2	3	4	5
18.	I was satisfied with my salary.	1	2	3	4	5
19.	I received adequate support (materials, resources, facilities, etc.) from the company.	1	2	3	4	5
20.	I did not always find the company's promotion policy a fair one.	1	2	3	4	5

21. I did not have easy access to my supervisor/manager.   1   2   3   4   5

22. My supervisor/manager treated me fairly.   1   2   3   4   5

23. My supervisor/manager supported me adequately.   1   2   3   4   5

24. My supervisor/manager was generally sensitive to the needs of subordinates.   1   2   3   4   5

25. My supervisor/manager was open and willing to aid me in planning a career path.   1   2   3   4   5

26. My supervisor/manager let me know when my work was satisfactory.   1   2   3   4   5

27. My supervisor/manager made every effort to be fair with me regarding pay increases.   1   2   3   4   5

THE VALUE
OF EMPLOYEE COMMENTS

The fourth page of the questionnaire (Exhibit 2) provides space in which employees can write comments. If they do not fear identification or reprisals, experience indicates that 10 to 20 percent will write suggestions or complaints that they feel have not been adequately covered by the other questions. In a first survey, 10 percent of employees will usually comment. Subsequent surveys will usually elicit a greater number of comments.

Here are some comments from surveys made by Benge Associates:

- We need a first aid kit for use by the night shift.

- The boss drinks on the job; after a few hours he doesn't make sense.

- Rejects are much greater than shown on the Daily Report.

- When the quality inspector isn't looking, workers often dump rejects into the "approved" bin.

- The foreman tells me one thing, the superintendent something else. Either way, I get bawled out. I'm about ready to quit.

- I suggest that the Time Sheet and Production Report be combined to avoid a lot of duplication.

Comments on this part of the survey often alert management to possible trouble:

- A group leader was a drug addict.

- A supervisor on the night shift was reported to be sleeping during working hours. When confronted, he said he also had a day job: "I had to get some sleep somewhere, and couldn't do it on my day job."

- In an oil distribution company, a truck driver had rigged a small motor that pumped air into the line. When the oil meter registered 500 gallons delivered, the homeowner actually received less than 400. The truck driver used the "saved" oil to heat his own home.

- A union official, visiting the workers on the night shift at a plant, regularly took a case of canned goods out the back door and put it in his car.

Management must be extremely careful about the way it uses information obtained from employee comments. Managers especially have come under increasing fire recently as targets of employee disenchantment. We are living in an age of employee litigation. Disciplinary actions that only a decade ago were considered standard operating procedure in non-union shops are now often considered unfair. They frequently result in legal actions that are costly even when management is found in court to be blameless.

ANALYZING EMPLOYEE COMMENTS

Employee comments should be typed exactly as written, including misspellings and bad grammar. We repeat: the questionnaires should *not* be shown to company executives. To do so would violate the confidentiality promised by the survey administrator.

Often, comments deal with the desire for higher pay. This may indicate a need for management to compare its wage levels with those of other employers in the community, to install a wage and salary administration, or to improve the salary system now in use. However, it may also call for job evaluation within the company to ensure that equitable treatment is given to various classifications of jobs. If wage incentives are not subject to a union contract or government rules, then some form of incentive pay might be considered to make higher earnings possible without increasing unit costs.

Some suggestions made by employees will be economically unfeasible, of course, but even these should not be ignored. In subsequent reporting to employees in the company newspaper, newsletter, memorandums, or meetings, economically unfeasible suggestions should be revealed, and the reasons given for the company not being able to implement them. Note, though, that the exact comment should not be reported, just the general idea.

Some suggestions can be quickly implemented, such as better lighting, cleaner rest rooms, safety guards, and noise control. When such changes are made, they should be publicized, with credit given to employees for making the suggestion.

Quick response to suggestions made by employees has a favorable impact on morale.

SELECTED EMPLOYEE COMMENTS

Sometimes minor employee irritants can easily be corrected. Here are a few examples from the Company X survey:

- The workers in the warehouse complained about mice. A cat solved the problem.

- Employees in the machine shop wanted some way to keep milk cold. Management provided the materials for the employees to build a cooling chest using a bypass from the drinking-water system.

- Employees in one plant complained that the first floor was always too hot, the second floor too cold. Vents between floors relieved both conditions.

- An office employee wrote, "Two of us need larger desks because of the volume of papers we handle, but the office is too small." Management had a tier of shelves built on top of each desk, which removed the paper clutter from the desktops.

- Employees commented that medical aid was poor. Yet management had recently purchased excellent medical aid equipment. Investigation showed that most employees needed instruction in using first aid equipment. Instruction was introduced.

A SELECTION
OF FINDINGS FROM
144 SURVEYS

When capable management consultants conduct the entire survey, they can usually make useful recommendations. Otherwise, the survey administrator conducts the survey through the statistical phase and presents the data to management. Then a top management committee studies the data and prepares recommendations. Analyzing employee comments should be done by high-level management.

This chapter presents a selection of findings from 144 surveys conducted by Benge Associates and the resulting recommendations. The findings and recommendations came from analyses of morale indices, percentages, and employee comments. You can use these data to gain insight into typical problems you may discover.

Going Outside the Company to Fill Vacancies

In a number of these surveys employees' comments showed that they believed that management filled vacancies for good jobs with outsiders. Here is how three companies met this situation:

- The president of a paper manufacturing company ordered a study made of the last hundred job vacancies at all levels. To his dismay, he learned that although 90 percent of salaried jobs had been filled by internal promotions, only 47 percent of hourly-paid job vacancies had been filled internally. Hence there was considerable merit to the employees' complaints. The president ordered that announcements of all vacancies above starting jobs be posted on bulletin boards. Employees who asked to be considered for promotion to these jobs were to be tested by the personnel department and interviewed by the prospective supervisor. The selection was to be approved by the next higher-level manager.

- The second company, in the furniture business, took a different course. It instituted an annual search for talent, during which employees volunteered to take aptitude tests administered by an impartial management consultant. This procedure regularly discovered previously unknown talent. In addition, it enabled management to say to complaining employees, "Get in on the next search for talent."

- The third company's management determined that employees' feelings about lack of internal promotions were unjustified. In the employee newspaper it listed all job vacancies above starting level that had been filled internally, along with those that had been filled from the outside. Names of employees were shown. The list of internally appointed employees contained sixty-six names; the outsider-appointment list, eight names. Each month thereafter the newspaper presented similar information. The publicity had two effects: it showed employees the true status of internal promotions versus outside hiring, and it caused supervisors to search more carefully for inside personnel to promote.

Too Many Bosses

Many employees in a plant producing intricate electronic equipment commented that they often received orders from two or more persons and that these directions often contradicted each other. A study showed that laboratory scientists and quality control inspectors did indeed cut across one another in order to meet difficult customer specifications or deadlines. A management consultant recommended that staff scientists write out changes they wanted and get the superintendent to resolve conflicting orders before giving them to employees.

The Boss Who Didn't Boss

In one department of a soft drink bottler where production costs were high, the foreman was well liked. But employees' attitudes toward their jobs, toward the company, and toward management were very negative. Investigation revealed that the workers received virtually no supervision; they simply did as they pleased. Management corrected this problem by teaching the foreman how to lead and supervise.

Wage Inequity

In a large paper mill, management learned from a survey that foremen's attitudes toward their earnings were negative, even more negative than those of the production employees.

Investigation showed that several machine tenders, who received a great deal of overtime pay, were earning more than their foremen. Management instituted a bonus plan that made it possible for foremen to earn at least 15 percent more each quarter than the average of their three highest paid subordinates. Production increased and spoilage decreased.

Food for Employees

Employees in a textile mill registered strong disapproval of food, service, and prices in the plant cafeteria, which was already losing money for the company. Management shut down the kitchen, contracted with a concessionaire to install food-dispensing machines, and donated the net proceeds from the concession to the employees' athletic fund. A majority of employees approved the change.

Resolving Conflicting Demands

Management is sometimes faced with conflicting demands. In a small steel plant, for example, younger employees repeatedly suggested to management that retirement at a certain age be made compulsory. At the same time, however, older employees opposed the idea. To solve this conflict, management asked questions about it in a morale survey. Employees voted overwhelmingly against mandatory retirement.

In another shop, employees complained so bitterly about the foreman that he quit. Management wanted to promote a bright young man with low seniority, but feared that the older employees would resent such a move. In an attempt to elicit workers' opinions, management asked forty-seven employees to designate in order their three choices for the job, on secret ballots. The young man management favored received thirty-eight first-place votes and was thereupon promoted to foreman. This was an unusual solution to a problem at the time it occurred, but nowadays, when an increasing number of companies are owned by their employees, promotions by election are certain to increase.

Employee Councils

Based on findings of morale surveys conducted by Benge Associates, two companies formed employee councils to which employees elected their own representatives. These councils considered complaints, offered suggestions for improvements, and made recommendations to management. Workers considered it an honor to be elected to the council. Moreover, radically minded employees, when faced with management problems as members of the council, soon toned down their radical views.

Unsolvable Problems

Drivers for a nationwide bus transportation system complained through a survey that they had little opportunity for advancement. The statement was true. There were few higher paid jobs, and the drivers were based in many localities all over the country. To improve morale the company offered to help drivers find better jobs in other companies. However, because of their high earnings, few of them quit.

Community Relations

In one rural community, the large plant of a national paper manufacturing company overshadowed a small local textile mill. A survey of the employees of the small mill revealed that they took little pride in their company. Management decided to pay employees for one month in silver dollars.

These unusual coins soon flooded the local stores and services, making people realize that the small company was an important force in the town's economy. Employee pride went up.

Overcoming Resistance to Mechanization

A manufacturer of heavy electrical cable, employing almost four hundred workers, was considering the purchase of automated equipment that would displace ninety workers over a two-year period. Because employees had resisted new machine installations, the directors were apprehensive about the proposed purchase. They included this question in a survey: "If the company were to put in more labor-saving machinery, which of the following do you think would happen?" Five choices for answers were provided. The final report showed that 11 percent had checked negative answers, 11 percent had revealed some uncertainty, and an overwhelming 78 percent had expressed faith that the company would offer other work for displaced employees. Based on this result, the company installed the equipment and announced that it would see that all employees affected would be reassigned to other work. The company's action forestalled a potentially serious morale problem.

Increasing Job Satisfaction

A baking company had plants in four large cities employing a total of thirteen hundred workers. A survey showed that the main plant, which sold at wholesale only, suffered the lowest morale and profits. The other three plants sold largely to industrial employers from a fleet of small trucks. When management realized it had a morale problem, it promptly added a retail division to the home plant. Two years later, a repeat survey confirmed the wisdom of the move: morale at the main plant was on the same level as it was in the other three plants.

Reorganizing Management

A large steel corporation conducted surveys of supervisors at only three of its plants. These findings shocked top management:

- Of the supervisors, 59 percent said they did not have enough authority to discharge their responsibilities.

- Of the employees, 47 percent said they took orders from two or more superiors.

- At one plant, 79 percent of the employees rated the plant manager as very poor.

- One foreman said he didn't report to anyone.

The directors hired an independent consultant to interview all supervisors, guaranteeing them anonymity. Drastic changes in plant management practices resulted.

Enriching Jobs

A rapidly growing manufacturer of complex instruments employed about eighty instrument assemblers. When the owners decided to set up a production line, dissension soon surfaced. A morale survey showed that many technicians objected to performing a single operation instead of assembling a complete instrument. Management solved the problem by establishing three groups for subassemblies and one for final assembly. Each group soon evolved its own version of a production assembly line.

Not all these examples will be applicable to your situation, but they can serve as idea instigators for you. Be on the lookout for similar actions and programs that you read or hear about. Keep track of the best ideas in a notebook. They will add concreteness to your own efforts and suggestions.

RECOMMENDATIONS
AND MANAGEMENT ACTIONS

At some point, analyses and findings must be translated into recommendations for management actions. Such recommendations can be developed by administrators with previous experience, by a committee of senior company executives, or by joint consideration of both. Or they may be developed by a managers' task force led by you. If you've been involved throughout, offered cogent analyses, and spearheaded the implementation, this is an opportunity to show your leadership qualities.

COMPANY X RECOMMENDATIONS

When Company X moved to a larger building, there was considerable jockeying for the most favorable workspace in the new plant among department heads and employees. In addition, the plant manager, who was much disliked, had recently been removed by the board of directors. The directors wanted to learn employees' opinions about the new plant manager; they also wanted a basis for comparison of his success in employee relations for the future, when a repeat survey was planned.

An outside consultant made recommendations on employee selection, training, compensation, supervision, fringe benefits, and personnel policies, as well as these specific recommendations:

- Give the new plant manager more authority to handle complaints, authorize overtime, add to the work force, and approve wage increases.

- Promote a foreman to manager of production planning and scheduling.

- Ask the foremen to help devise individual performance standards against which their effectiveness could be judged.

- Have foremen meet weekly on company time to discuss a series of twelve booklets on better kinds of supervision.

- Buy or rent the adjoining empty lot to provide more parking space for all employees.

- Study layout and flow of work in the manual assembly department to find ways to relieve congestion and stop the existing dissension.

- Install overhead heaters in the shipping department.

- Install exhaust fans in the plating department.

- Have the night superintendent inspect housekeeping and machine maintenance at the close of the night shift.

RECOMMENDATIONS FROM SURVEYS

Here are brief recommendations selected from some reports to management based on recent surveys. In the reports, each recommendation is explained in detail so that management clearly understands the reasons for it and how it should be applied. Recommendations stem from statistical analyses, employee comments, and social or legislative trends pertinent to the survey findings.

1. Develop additional sources of labor supply.

2. Prepare job specifications to guide the employment interviewer.

3. Give physical examinations before accepting new employees.

4. Contact former employers of applicants being considered for jobs in grade 2 and higher.

5. Assign sponsors in each department to help orient and train new employees.

6. Post all job vacancies at all plants.

7. Interview new employees one week after they begin working.

8. Prepare and issue charts showing requirements for promotions to jobs in grades 2, 3, and 4.

9. Help establish a course in electronics in the local school.

10. Have the personnel and industrial engineering departments determine which jobs lend themselves to job enrichment.

11. Identify promotable employees and give them further training.

12. Offer a free eyesight examination to all employees.

13. Review and revise job titles based on job analysis.

14. Bring a job evaluation plan up to date.

15. Annually review living allowances for representatives stationed in foreign countries.

16. Improve lighting in the assembly and final inspection departments.

17. Install an asphalt surface in the employees' parking lot.

18. Appoint an ombudsman to whom employees can take their complaints.

19. Instruct supervisors in motivation and keep them apprised of the latest findings in industrial psychology.

20. Annually reeducate employees on sickness, hospital, and insurance benefits program.

21. Revise vacation policy so that it will be in line with community practice.

22. Award length-of-service pins for five, ten, and twenty years' service.

23. Encourage employees to help solve job problems at all levels.

24. Establish a varied program of recognition for outstanding performance.

25. Establish departmental committees to recommend or institute improvements.

IMPLEMENTING AN IMPROVEMENT PROGRAM

An attitude, opinion, or morale survey is not an end in itself.

Often managers feel that by conducting a survey they have allowed workers to air their complaints and that ill feelings will therefore disappear. On the contrary, in the absence of action, employees with complaints, justified or not, will feel that the survey was a farce, and poor attitudes may intensify.

The process of agreeing on an improvement program is, in itself, an education to the managers involved, but it is not enough for them merely to agree on a series of corrective measures. They must reach agreement on an improvement program, have it approved by the officers of the company, and work toward getting it in force by the completion dates.

REPORT TO EMPLOYEES

Most companies issue some form of report to employees, giving the overall results of most items on the survey. Some companies present the findings in a series of articles in the employees' newspaper; others issue a series of bulletins. A number of concerns print attractive four-page folders, in two colors, with bar charts. A few lighten the graphic presentation with sketches or cartoons.

Whatever form of reporting you choose, keep two things in mind:

(1) the report must be honest; and

(2) actions must follow.

PART II

Whether you're currently in a position to incorporate the survey techniques from Part I into your function or not, you can still incorporate modern motivational techniques into your management style, and you can do it today. Many companies have adopted a philosophy of management that allows workers greater freedom to determine how to get their work done, shared responsibility for results, greater discretion in choosing their work hours, and increased involvement—all of which contribute to an improvement in the quality of their work lives and to increased employee productivity.

Part II covers a wide spectrum of motivational techniques, suggestions, and examples. It blends theory with reality, giving you the why and how of individual and collective motivation situations.

From the psychological to the physical and all the stepping stones in between, this section offers advice from recognized experts, advice that you can use immediately. It focuses on actual problems such as motivating ineffective employees. It covers new psychotherapeutic techniques for counseling subordinates, as well as time-tested methods to generate new enthusiasm in your secretary.

You choose the specialized intelligence from these chapters that is applicable to your particular situation. Combine this information with your instinctive abilities to set the stage for the creation of a motivational management style all your own—one that will motivate your employees to greater productivity and make them, and you, more valuable to your firm.

KEYS
TO MOTIVATION

"Three simple keys are necessary to unlock the door to human progress within the workplace: care, continuous feedback, and the feeling of mutual need," said steelworker Donald Dalena in an article that appeared ten years ago in *Industry Week*. He continued this way:

> Care is a mirror, its output accurately reflecting the input. Managers who manifest care will eliminate stress, promote trust and improve attitude and morale.
>
> Feedback... What we would like to know is our competitive standing with our customers, where the product has come from, what happens to it after it leaves us, its planned future use and current problems connected with its production which influence our work lives in one form or another.
>
> The main ingredient lacking... is the feeling of mutual need. Top managers have not observed a simple fact: Each worker is there because he wants to work.... If the company's managers reacted equally—by recognizing that they hired a worker for a job because they needed a worker for

the job—and based their supervisory philosophy accordingly, many problems would vanish.

A decade later, Dalena's remarks are still significant on at least two counts. First, they reveal how different the attitudes of today's workers are from those of only a generation or so ago; the power of management to command or coerce has been lost. Second, they reveal the workers' awareness of their importance to the company.

FROM COERCION TO MOTIVATION

Concern about motivation of workers is a comparatively recent development. It has only been a generation since the studies of behavioral scientists began to prove that internal motivation is more effective than coercion. Internal motivation is self-sustaining, and it does not produce the resentment and frustration associated with coercion.

You may have noticed the change yourself. Today's workers question rather than carry out. Orders no longer produce immediate action. The traditional KITA (kick in the [pants]) theory has lost its steam. You need new techniques to craft a highly productive and motivated staff.

Douglas McGregor in *The Human Side of Enterprise* (New York: McGraw-Hill, 1960) suggested two choices for managing workers. His Theory X held that people are lazy, dislike work, and have to be driven to do their tasks; his Theory Y assumes that people have a psychological need to work, that they want to achieve and to be responsible, provided the job is rewarding and offers some freedom to use initiative.

Evidence to support McGregor's Theory Y appears in the works of other well-known theorists. See, for example,

Abraham Maslow, *Motivation and Personality* (New York: Harper & Row, 1954); Frederick Herzberg, *The Motivation to Work* (New York: Wiley, 1959); and David McClelland, *Motivating Economic Achievement* (New York: Free Press, 1969).

At the same time, however, these studies make it clear that the adoption of Theory Y as a philosophy of management would not by itself get satisfactory results. Indeed, the use of Theory Y as a guiding principle puts greater stress and responsibility on both managers and workers. The studies and experiences of these theorists and other behavioral scientists show that management's attempts to motivate workers depend on the factors enumerated below.

Workers and Their Needs

Among the factors that managers must consider when trying to improve motivation are the desires and needs of the individual workers. Today, workers are less eager for increased economic rewards and more interested in work as a means of self-fulfillment. This has been a natural outcome, even in the less developed parts of the world, of the growing numbers of people whose needs for physical comfort (food, shelter, and clothing) have been largely filled. Higher levels of education, an increase in sophistication, and increased worker mobility have also contributed to this increased emphasis on achieving self-fulfillment. In other words, many workers crave job satisfaction. People who get satisfaction from their jobs often sustain high-quality performance even when they are disappointed with their compensation, job security, or working conditions. But those who are bored and who get little or no emotional satisfaction from what they're doing will sooner or later become unreliable, prone to absenteeism, or ineffective as workers.

How to Determine Job Satisfaction Potential

The management consulting firm of Roy W. Walters & Associates of Ridgewood, New Jersey, has identified nine features by which you can recognize the satisfaction potential of a job. The checklist shown in Exhibit 5 is developed from them. Although the characteristics of certain jobs make it nearly impossible for them to give fulfillment, you can use this list to help reduce dissatisfaction in even the most difficult, monotonous, or tightly structured jobs.

Think about how many of these features apply to the people under your supervision. In fact, think about how many apply to you in your current situation!

CRITERIA FOR JOB DESIGNS THAT PROVIDE MOTIVATION

The founder of efficiency engineering, Frederick W. Taylor, proved at the turn of the century that breaking down tasks into small, repetitive steps was an efficient way to design manufacturing jobs. The best-known illustration of this concept is the assembly line, where a worker's only task may be to tighten a bolt on one identical part after another. The same kind of thinking has been applied to clerical and other nonmanufacturing work.

This fragmentation of tasks almost ensures monotony in jobs, with resulting lack of motivation. Until recently, however, instead of changing the design of jobs to increase work satisfaction, both management and labor have emphasized satisfactions outside the job itself—better pay, retirement benefits, and shorter hours, rather than elimination of unsatisfying work design.

EXHIBIT 5

Checklist for Measuring a Job's Satisfaction Potential

☐   The job doesn't seem monotonous to workers, but allows them to change pace by varying tasks.

☐   This job does not waste employees' time and effort, because management has planned the work in such a way that employees can do it without exerting energy uselessly.

☐   The workers feel free to plan their own work and the way they can do it most effectively.

☐   They believe they have a reasonable degree of authority over how the work should be done.

☐   Workers believe they have opportunities for individual recognition and growth in their jobs.

☐   They don't feel too closely supervised, overinstructed, or too rigidly controlled.

☐   Employees see their work as an integral part of the work of the whole company, and each worker as an individual, not merely a cog in a machine.

☐   The answer to the question, "How am I doing?" comes from the job itself; thus workers can correct their own errors and improve their own techniques.

☐   The job offers feedback from superiors without inducing embarrassment or attention.

Those who advocate redesigning jobs also favor higher pay and and shorter hours, but they claim that these rewards alone will not motivate workers to superior performance. They believe that motivation must come from workers and the work itself.

Job designs that provide motivation should meet these criteria:

- *Naturally identifiable units of work.* In a ten-step assembly process, a typical job arrangement might have each step performed by a separate worker. In manufacturing, for example, one worker might spot-weld all day long on one part of a product. In purchasing, a clerk might have the single task of telephoning suppliers to check on the status of overdue orders of one class of supplies. In both instances, the workers are performing small, isolated tasks rather than complete jobs. To build motivation into such jobs, management can redesign them so that workers perform a number of tasks instead of only the one. For example, manufacturing workers can assemble entire products or components, either by themselves or as part of a team. Purchasing clerks can be given responsibility for several classes of purchases—for example, maintenance, repair, and operating supplies. Their tasks could be broadened, allowing them to solicit bids, compare prices, select sources, issue purchase orders, and expedite deliveries. Both changes will allow workers to identify with and take pride in the company's larger activities and goals.

- *"Client" relationships.* The logical grouping of tasks and the worker's accountability for them should be the basis of a relationship with other persons who are "clients" for the worker's services.

- *Job module design.* The job must be structured to give the worker both variety and autonomy. The first principle of job module design is "horizontal loading"—widening the scope of the task to provide the worker with variety, thus increasing the stimulation he or she can derive from the work. The second principle of job module design is "vertical loading"—expanding the basic job module by adding more challenging tasks, greater responsibility, and more self-supervision, autonomy, and control.

- *Feedback systems*. Workers should regularly receive information about their performance from "clients" (the persons being dealt with), from the supervisor, and from standards of performance built into the job itself. This feedback lets workers know how well they are meeting the requirements of the job. It also reinforces good performance and provides a basis for self-correction of errors.

- *Task advancement*. Jobs should offer opportunities for workers to increase their skills and knowledge, to win recognition and advancement. In addition to this, a job should offer the workers a chance to increase their work responsibilities.

You will shoulder more and more responsibility as you move up the corporate ladder, and your subordinates should do likewise. Increasing workers' responsibility will have a dual effect: you'll help accomplish your primary objective, motivation; you'll also extend your influence and get more done in less time and with less effort.

OBSTACLES TO MOTIVATION

The relationships between supervisors and subordinates and among peers can contribute to the motivational climate within an organization. Relationships work positively or negatively depending on their nature. Many relationships are based on historical precedents.

If management says to workers, "This is the way we have always done things in this company," it implies that it does not care for the employees as human beings. Instead, management regards them as nothing but cogs in the production machine.

John Zenger, of Zenger, Miller and Associates, Menlo Park, California, believes that internal motivation can result from the removal of obstacles to productive work. One obstacle is senseless company policies that persist when management lacks the determination to rid the company of them.

Another obstacle to internal motivation is bad supervision.

A company that promotes good workers to supervisors without training them in human relations, for example, is asking for poor supervision. Dr. Zenger points out that many supervisors grow up in an authoritative atmosphere, give orders without explanation, and are impatient with workers who bring up matters such as boredom, pointless work, or lack of opportunity. In fact, such supervisors often show contempt for suggestions from workers. Their attitudes effectively destroy the average individual's desire to do a good job.

A third obstacle to motivation is the bureaucratic organizational structure of many companies. The structure frustrates attempts to make changes, no matter how beneficial they may appear to be. It also destroys communication because the bureaucracy talks but seldom listens. Managers who do not listen appear to care nothing about people below them in the organization hierarchy.

The Group as a Dynamic Force for Motivation

"Managers should concentrate on organizing the work group into an instrument of cooperation," Dr. Zenger says. "The group is the strongest force we know of today for influencing individual members. To be effective, managers must learn to use the group effectively. Most problems relating to productivity and motivation exist because the group itself is carelessly organized and directed due to management's failure to clarify goals, make the mission of the group clear and listen attentively about the day-to-day problems that arise," Dr. Zenger concludes.

In most organizations industrial engineers have been the designers of jobs. Their objective has been to create jobs that require the least amount of time, motion, and thought. Reducing the human element, industrial engineers believe, lessens chances for error. What the industrial engineers have done, however, is to design jobs that frustrate workers.

Only recently have behavioral scientists spoken out on the subject of designing jobs to be meaningful and rewarding to the workers. Their theories have now moved from the laboratories to shop floors and offices.

Dr. Zenger also believes that the problem of the boring job that cannot be eliminated or automated can be solved. It calls for nothing more complicated than frequent rotation, something that only the Japanese have adopted to any extent. "An excellent example of the value of job rotation," Dr. Zenger says, "is the McDonald's hamburger fast food outlets. Jobs in this company at the blue-collar level are all potentially boring. But McDonald's is an extremely efficient operation with employees who are generally pleasant to customers, happy at their jobs, and quite conscientious about doing their work well. McDonald's rotates people with incredible frequency from one routine job to another. I do not think most workers spend more than an hour at one task before moving to another. Each job by itself is monotonous, but with such rapid rotation, the individual seldom has the time to get bored before moving to another."

Rewards and Incentives as Means of Motivation

Many behavioral scientists have placed low values on monetary rewards as motivational factors. Frederick Herzberg, for example, points out that as the need for economic rewards lessens, they no longer serve as incentives. Then they become "hygiene factors." Herzberg believes that when workers become unhappy or dissatisfied with such rewards, they then become demotivators.

This seems to confirm Abraham Maslow's "hierarchy of needs." All human needs, Maslow says, ascend from the first level, at which people require food, shelter, and clothing; when this need is filled, workers begin to ask for safety and security; then, when that need is filled, they move on to the desire to belong, to be accepted; their next wish is to enjoy esteem and reputation. At the top of Maslow's hierarchy is self-actualization, or fulfillment. Rewards can be devised to motivate people to attain each level in the hierarchy of needs. Once a level of need has been reached, however, its rewards no longer provide continuing motivation.

While economic rewards do have power to motivate, they also contain risk. Workers can compare the amount of money they receive to the amounts their peers inside or outside the company get. They can see and compare money rewards more easily than other motivators. Thus, what they perceive to be fair pay one day they may regard as unfair (a disincentive) the next if their peers achieve additional pay increases. That is a crucial reason why systems of money rewards must be carefully and properly managed.

Look at your own monetary situation. Every person's ideal is to combine vocation and avocation, and get paid well in the process. But few reach such a station in their work life. This cynical maxim is just as true for your employees as it is for you: money talks. But it is not the only sound that provides motivation.

TRAINING AS A MOTIVATOR

Training is so much a part of any job that it is frequently overlooked as the powerful motivator that it can be. Peter Drucker points out that the Japanese method of making workers take responsibility for their jobs and their tools is continuous training. All employees at every level keep on training until they retire. Weekly training sessions are regular and scheduled parts of their work. The sessions are usually conducted by the employees and supervisors themselves rather than by a trainer. Drucker says,

> Continuous training gives every worker a knowledge of his own performance, of his own standards, and . . . [of the performance of] other fellow workers on his level. It creates the habit of looking at "our work." It creates a community of working and workers. . . . The individual employee tends to see beyond the boundaries of his own specialty and his own department. He knows what goes on. He knows the work of others. He sees the genuine whole and he is expected to be concerned with the performance of every single job in this genuine whole. He, therefore, can see his own place in the structure and his own contribution.

Training can meet some of the desires of workers, as expressed in the quotation at the beginning of Chapter 9: "care, continuous feedback, and the feeling of mutual need"—of the company for the worker and the worker for the company.

Not everyone wants to advance and take on additional responsibilities. Yet no one wants to be in a position where there are no opportunities for development. To block workers' growth is to place limitations on their freedom to act; it removes possibilities for recognition; it takes away their freedom to plan their work, to change their work, to vary their pace, to learn how well they are doing. Without any opportunity to develop, workers can only conclude that the company does not care about them, that there is no "feeling of mutual need." Restraints on opportunities for self-development are obstacles to internal motivation. Management should remove them and make it clear to workers that this company encourages and provides opportunities for development.

MOTIVATION THROUGH COMMUNICATION

Concern for the morale, enthusiasm, and effectiveness of your employees must not be a short-term or one-shot deal. It should arise from an ongoing, long-range communications system that keeps management aware of what employees are thinking, what their attitudes are, how they feel about their jobs, their managers, their working conditions, and so on. In short, you must be able to keep your fingers on the "motivational pulse" continually. A system of motivation through communication begins with teaching management at all levels to be aware of those factors that are measures

of true motivation as well as those that are simply job satisfiers.

Job satisfiers are those things the company provides to
recruit and maintain high-caliber employees. Some job satisfiers are salary, benefits, job security, working conditions, company policies, and social relationships. These job
satisfiers are very important in their own right and in re-
cruiting and maintaining good people, but they do not by
themselves promote productivity. It has been found, for
example, that a salary increase increases productivity for
only a short period of time.

The real motivators are those factors that truly increase
productivity—feelings that workers have about their jobs.
Here are some examples:

- My work has value, so I'm valuable.

- This is challenging work, and I'm doing it well.

- There's a good chance I'll be noticed if I do a good
job.

- I am getting better at this job.

- I am responsible for what does and doesn't happen.

Knowing and understanding what truly motivates workers will help you develop and implement programs that can
positively influence employees' feelings and thereby increase productivity. These programs are usually based on a
series of communications that help management to measure
and react to the workers' feelings. One such communication
is the morale survey discussed in Part I.

The environment in which internal motivation can thrive
and be self-sustaining must exist throughout an organization, at every level and in all areas of the company. This

motivational environment is as important to organizations as it is to individuals. Business is finding it increasingly difficult to grow in the face of economic fluctuations, government regulations, and political and environmental constraints. The substitution of capital or technological innovation for labor is no longer a guarantee of progress. Utilizing the human resource in a humane and effective way is currently the most promising method for organizations to keep moving ahead.

And it is a most promising way for you to keep moving ahead as well. Setting the pace in motivation innovation at your firm can help stamp the "can't miss" label on your career.

THE MOTIVATING ENVIRONMENT

A motivating environment contains a combination of good physical conditions and positive mental attitudes. The dominance of one over the other will depend on the workers' perception of the nature and importance of the work they do. Workers can perform extremely well under atrocious conditions when their desire to achieve is strong. Conversely, the best possible conditions will not prevent them from doing inferior work if they simply don't want to achieve.

In other words, truly motivated people can accomplish wonders in dreadful environments. Consider, for example, the amazing engineering feats accomplished by prisoners of war in their attempts to escape. Without tools and despite darkness, danger, constant interruptions, and the threat of discovery, prisoners constructed elaborate tunnels, designed and installed complicated ventilation systems, and arranged for the disposal of tons of displaced earth without being discovered. Highly motivated, the prisoners did not allow a bad working environment to stop them from accomplishing their objectives. They were, it is true, well led by individuals who provided clear directions and the constant encouragement that human beings desire under any conditions. Good leadership helps overcome a bad environment.

PHYSICAL FACTORS

Some kinds of work, however, simply cannot be performed efficiently when the physical environment is inadequate. Let's say, for example, that several workers have the task of sorting many small objects of slightly different shades of green. Let's also say that the work station is poorly lighted. In this situation—no matter how well the supervisors train the workers, no matter how many incentives are given for accuracy—the workers will make numerous errors. The bad light is an obstacle to performance, workers will quickly lose interest in the task, and soon they will not even try to do a good job. For this group of workers and this kind of job, the physical conditions of work cannot be overcome. The environment has demotivated the employees.

Compare this situation with the working environment of steelworkers. They usually work in a noisy, hot, and dangerous place, but they expect these conditions and do not consider them unusual. If they have the proper tools, and if the arrangement of the workplace lets them do the job with a minimum of interference, they consider their environment adequate. They do not expect carpets on the floor, air conditioning, or soft music. If management suggested such amenities, the steelworkers would be astonished and amused. They accept their environment because it is conducive to accomplishing the type of work they do and because the physical factors are exactly what the workers expect them to be.

Leadership can do much to overcome obstacles created by an unsatisfactory working environment, however. Consider this example of an actual aluminum foundry. It was hot, dirty, and noisy. The air was saturated with fine particles of oil. The wooden framework of the building frequently caught fire from the heat of the furnaces, adding danger to discomfort. However, this company's aerospace products had a reputation for excellence and were used in many critical applications where human life was at risk. The workers were highly motivated, interested in the quality of the product they made, and not much disturbed by the poor conditions of their workplace. What gave them this desire to achieve?

The managers of this plant were proud of their work force and showed how much they cared about them. They made sure that each worker knew the purposes of the products, where they went after they left the factory, and how they were used in airplanes and spacecraft. Management brought factory representatives of the companies that bought the products into the plant to tell the workers how their excellent workmanship contributed to safety and performance.

As a result, workers took pride in their accomplishments and felt a responsibility to do well. They knew what their work was achieving and felt that they were being recognized for it. They had feedback from the company's clients and could see their work as an important part of the end product. The inferior quality of their physical environment, therefore, had little effect on their attitudes toward their jobs, and this obstacle was overcome by good leadership.

In this foundry, management recognized the inadequacy of the workplace. But the company could not afford to improve physical conditions. Management explained to the workers that the company had recently been purchased by a larger organization. The new owners planned to buy the adjacent land for a major expansion and did not feel that radical remodeling of the existing facilities would be economical. Management promised that the company would make some improvements in the present plant as soon as possible, however.

The company also began an intensive campaign to improve safety. It hired a nurse to care for minor injuries, installed equipment to filter particles from the air, and purchased jump tanks—large tanks of fresh water into which workers could plunge if their clothing caught fire or they got splashed with acid.

The foundry workers, knowing that their managers had never deceived them, did not ask for or expect the impossible. The caring attitude of management encouraged cooperation. Workers reciprocated by producing at peak efficiency.

DETERMINING WHEN TO MAKE PHYSICAL IMPROVEMENTS

Improvement of the workplace will not by itself motivate workers. It is doubtful, for example, that the construction of the new plant will improve the attitudes of the workers in the aluminum foundry. Failure to build a new plant after promising to do so, however, would have a devastating effect on morale and would result in demotivation. The new foundry should increase productivity, though, because of the convenience of working in a better designed area. Reduction of the discomforts and fire hazards should let workers produce more.

Management needs to examine the effects of the physical plant on output. Then it should observe the workers' and the managers' attitudes. If, on the one hand, the attitude of management is conducive to internal motivation, but the environmental obstacles are so great that they overwhelm all attempts at improving production, then physical changes should be implemented quickly. If, on the other hand, an uncaring attitude is the root problem, management can, for the moment, postpone improvements in the physical plant and concentrate on changing the attitudes of managers and of workers.

Donald Dalena, the steelworker quoted earlier, has this advice:

> Think small. Look for those seemingly infinitesimal and picayune frustrations that cumulatively produce stress and anxiety. Ferret them out and correct them. Stop fighting boredom and fight frustration. Treat the job holder as a person whose needs command as much attention as the machine he operates. Listen. Your workers are trying to tell you how to do a better job.

OTHER DEMOTIVATING CONDITIONS

Poor working conditions and negative attitudes are not the only demotivators that can block your attempts to create a productive work force. Any plan or system, financial or otherwise, can serve as a disincentive if it motivates an employee to work less effectively. Financial incentive plans that are perceived as unfair or unrealistic or that conflict with basic employee values also can demotivate workers.

Here are some disincentives to beware of as you create your motivation program:

- Promotion based on favoritism or seniority rather than on ability and accomplishment

- Failure to deal with employees' problems in a timely and constructive manner as they arise

- Encouraging employees to develop more efficient methods of performing their jobs and then using that information to cut out jobs

- Implementing a highly authoritarian style of management that induces tension and distrust

- Pay increases that come automatically with time and not with effectiveness

Part of your process of motivation should be to identify the disincentives over which you have control. If the executive vice-president your department reports to is a relative of Genghis Khan, there's not much you can do about it, but you can conduct a demotivation audit and develop appropriate action plans based on what you find. Besides finding ways to improve the motivation of your own people, you may come across some positive suggestions for the company as a whole. That will add another feather to your corporate hat.

One note to remember here: there is a difference between disincentives and negative incentives. While you're always striving to build positive incentives and motivation, as a practical matter, you must accept the existence of negative incentives in your program. Negative incentives are policies that *prevent* workers from doing certain things— arriving late, for instance. They needn't be punitive. You can instead structure them as corrective. For example, poorer performers can receive small or no salary increases; bonus awards can be smaller; or promotion opportunities can be withheld.

You must meld this corrective approach with effective communications. Tell your people what you expect of them and how their performance will affect their reward—or lack of reward.

THE MANAGER
AS PRIME MOTIVATOR

As we have seen, the environment can be a motivating or demotivating factor. Now we will see that individual characteristics and activities of the manager can serve the same purpose. You've undoubtedly developed some systems or programs of your own. The rest of Part II will give you many more good ideas to incorporate into your motivation activities. Two subjects are especially pertinent for today's progressive manager. One is a recent concept called psychotherapeutic management. The other is the age-old problem of employee deadwood.

USING PSYCHOTHERAPEUTIC TECHNIQUES TO IMPROVE PERFORMANCE

Donald Sanzotta, a professor of psychology and consultant to leading business firms, has written extensively about therapeutic management, which allows you to motivate your subordinates by becoming their mentor, or trusted counselor. Here are some basic principles:

• Start by recognizing people's strengths; then help them to recognize these strengths and develop their own abilities.

• Don't ignore weaknesses; help workers to recognize and correct their own weaknesses.

• Avoid treating subordinates like children; don't try to manipulate them or tell them what they must and must not do. Instead, treat them like adults. Motivate them to take the initiative in improving their performance for their own sake. Help them understand why they should follow the rules and procedures.

• Determine the best way to deal with each specific situation. You needn't always be docile or conciliatory. When necessary, assert yourself, exert control, and take strong, decisive stands.

• When you must disapprove or correct your employees, always aim at their behavior, never at them as persons. Always show regard for them. Never undermine their ego or self-esteem.

• Instead of blaming a person when something goes wrong, enlist the workers' cooperation in solving the problem. Try to depersonalize and defuse the issue by concentrating on what is right, not who is wrong.

• Always be honest, trustworthy, and straightforward, but don't always act the same in your dealings with subordinates. People's actions are strongly affected by their emotions, which vary with each individual. People also vary in their ability to express inner feelings and in their level of self-esteem. Become sensitive to these differences, which can guide your approach to each person.

Self-esteem as the Key

The key to successful therapeutic management is to support and enhance your subordinates' self-esteem and feeling of competence and confidence.

We all develop two concepts of ourselves—the ideal self (what we think we should be) and the real self (our perception of what we actually are). The smaller the gap between these two selves, the higher our self-esteem will be. The greater the gap, the lower will be our self-esteem. All kinds of self-defeating, neurotic behavior can result from low self-esteem. Dealing effectively with a person whose self-esteem is low often requires you to take a quite different approach than you would with a person who is very self-confident.

Psychologist Carl Rogers developed a simple test to measure the gap between the ideal self and the real self. He used a special deck of cards, each of which bore a different personal trait. First, people were asked to pick out the cards they thought applied to them. Then the deck was reshuffled and they chose the cards that showed traits they would like to have. The difference in the cards selected points to the real self–ideal self gap.

You can devise a test in which people separate their actual and ideal traits simply by asking such questions as these:

- Do you feel you're doing well here or should you be doing better?

- What would you really like to be doing?

- Do you get along with other people as well as you'd like to?

- Do you think you control your temper sufficiently or do you wish you could control it better?

- What aspects of your job would you like to handle better?

Also, you can often measure a person's self-esteem from casual conversation. Self-denigrating remarks such as "I don't know why I do that" or "I wish I didn't make so many mistakes" may be a good indication that the person lacks self-confidence.

Empathetic Listening

One of the most effective therapeutic management techniques is empathetic listening—not merely listening to people under you, but listening with genuine concern for their feelings. This is part of a nondirective approach that promotes trust between you and the person to whom you are listening while helping that person learn to accept his or her true self. Here are some guidelines:

- Let the other person do most of the talking.

- Don't try to diagnose, advise, or interpret what the other person says; just encourage him or her to think independently and to develop satisfactory answers to problems.

- Occasionally ask clarifying, open-ended questions.

- Give information regarding the problem.

- Never speculate about the person's subconscious motives.

- Approve, disapprove, guide, or correct the person's behavior while giving emotional support.

You need to be aware of the level of intimacy with which each worker is comfortable. Many people are afraid or unwilling to reveal how they truly feel. Getting them to trust you and reveal themselves to you takes time and patience.

Restating what people say, but in different words and without casting judgment on it, will help you gain insight into their feelings. But don't just echo what is said. Carl Rogers explains, "Try to see the world from [the other person's] vantage point."

The opportunity to express themselves often provides people with an emotional catharsis. They feel relief after talking out their problems. Sigmund Freud discovered that, if you let people talk, they will in time tell you everything you need to know about their problems. Directly or indirectly, their repressed feelings will come out. And just expressing repressed feelings can be very therapeutic. "Catharsis" is another term for a simple idea: "You'll feel better if you talk about it."

A WASTED ASSET

Deadwood employees—those workers who just go through the motions—are a problem every manager faces from time to time. Usually, these are employees who were once highly productive but who lost their motivation over time. Not only are they a burden on the company payroll and a slow point in operations, but they also represent a wasted asset. With their skills and experience, these individuals should be making an important contribution to the company. Instead, they have become extra weight.

Identifying Deadwood Employees

If you see an individual falling into a dull daily routine, now's the time to talk to him or her before the problem gets worse.

To help you identify those workers who are showing the first signs of becoming deadwood, here's a list of the signs and symptoms you should be aware of:

- Restlessness—The individual shows impatience on the job, in a meeting, in discussions, or when talking to you. The worker tends to watch the clock and looks forward only to weekends and holidays.

- Unpredictability—An employee decides to do things in an almost irrational manner, giving little thought to his or her actions, doing everything on impulse. "I just want to add a little excitement to my life" is the usual rationale.

- Missed deadlines—A worker not only misses them but grows defensive and shifts the blame to somebody else: "My report would have been done on time if only those people over in shipping had done their jobs on time!"

- Trivial appointments—Workers, particularly sales representatives, sometimes do this to keep up the pretense that they have a busy day. The day is full of meetings and appointments, but few of them lead to sales.

- Short attention span—Workers may appear to be bored with what you're saying or thinking about something else. If you ask, the reply is "Sure, boss, I know what you want me to do. I've done it a hundred times in the past."

- Failure to communicate—Sometimes older workers become alienated from younger co-workers, especially if many colleagues have left or retired early. They may be reluctant to join in with new associates. You might find them daydreaming about the "good old days."

* Negative attitude—This is often found in older workers who may feel that younger workers and new techniques don't add up to better productivity. These people may be reluctant to try new methods and techniques.

* Lack of interest in goals—"Whatever you want me to do, boss, I'll do it. That's what I get paid for." The attitude and the enthusiasm are lacking. These workers don't seem to care whether the project is completed or accomplished; they just do the work in a routine fashion.

* Frequent simple mistakes—This means that a worker is thinking about something else. The employee is starting to take everything for granted on the job and is no longer paying attention to the job at hand.

* Failure to follow up—This shows that individuals aren't really interested or involved in the growth or progress of the company. It is another indication that they do their work but no more; there's no enthusiasm or interest as to how the project turns out.

The First Step: Talk It Out

As soon as you recognize the deadwood syndrome in an employee, you should bring him or her in for an interview. To begin with, the worker may not be aware of the problem. Explain that his or her performance has not been up to par, but don't be overly critical. Put the emphasis on listening, on finding out how the person feels about the situation. Next, try to determine if there is a specific cause for the employee's slack performance—a grievance against the company perhaps, a marital or other personal problem, or an undisclosed illness. Finally, talk about what can be done to bring back full productivity. Focus on the person's strengths. How can the worker get more out of his or her skills? What insights has experience provided? Appeal to pride. The worker is capable of much more. How can you help him or her to achieve better?

Above all, take a positive, future-oriented attitude. The deadwood employee tends to paint past achievements in glowing colors but foresees the future in drab gray. Let the person know you have confidence in him or her. Picture the worker as more than just a body in the department. Instead, make all employees see themselves as important participants in the operation.

Four Sparks of Life

Here are four key ways to boost the productivity of dead-wood workers:

Feedback. The simplest and often the most effective cure for the deadwood syndrome is to let your employees know the company cares about them. A thank-you can be as important as a pay raise. Give a little more attention to those workers who seem to be slowing down. Let them know how their efforts fit into the company's goals. Be sure to praise a job well done. The deadwood phenomenon often begins after a worker performs particularly well and then feels the accomplishment has gone unnoticed.

Growth. Deadwood employees have stagnated. Push them to learn new skills, to investigate new methods of doing the job, to widen their horizons. For example, an office manager at one company had, after twenty-two years, fallen into a rut. When his superior suggested he begin looking into the possibility of an office conversion to word processing, the office manager went after the project wholeheartedly. He was able to apply his extensive practical knowledge and experience to the new techniques and procedures of the office of the future.

Employees who are learning and growing pick up skills that may be valuable to them in their careers. They also become revitalized and thus perform their regular duties with newfound enthusiasm.

Variety. If a complete change of assignments is not feasible, you can usually find a way to switch an employee into a new area temporarily. Task forces and committees are ideal vehicles for providing workers with a change of pace. Not only do they return to their regular duties refreshed, but they also gain new ideas to contribute to the problem at hand.

Self-management. Ideally, good workers need less guidance and supervision the longer they are on the job. Supervising them too tightly over the long run saps their initiative. A good way to revive enthusiasm is to let the experienced employees take a larger role in setting their own goals, scheduling their own work, and monitoring their own performance. In the best circumstances, self-management provides several advantages: it rekindles the employees' interest in their work, encourages them to find better ways to do the job, and lessens the workload of the supervisor.

12

MOTIVATING
SPECIFIC SEGMENTS OF
THE EMPLOYEE POPULATION

As you rise through the ranks of your company, you'll undoubtedly confront situations that call for individual motivating techniques. But you should also be aware of some general methods for treating certain types of employees. While certain motivations are universal, the shrewd manager recognizes that specific groups have specific "hot buttons."

Just as you wouldn't treat a shy individual the same way you'd treat an aggressive one, so you shouldn't try to motivate a technical subordinate, say, the same way you would a secretary.

The next two chapters concentrate on your interaction with four types of employee whom you'll have to motivate:

- Groups

- Failed subordinates

- Professionals

- Secretaries

MOTIVATING GROUPS

To conduct board meetings, planning conferences, problem-solving workshops, strategic development seminars, and even small meetings in your office, you must understand how to facilitate, influence, and motivate a group. If you cannot do this, you'll find yourself at a serious disadvantage.

How can you learn to work with groups? "It takes only three things," says Byron Eicher, an expert on group and organizational behavior, "awareness, awareness, and awareness."

Here is an example. An experienced manager with a respected work record was promoted to district director. At that time, his responsibilities changed from marketing products to overseeing the operation of several divisions, and he welcomed the opportunity and the challenge. Before assuming the position, he diligently studied the policies, procedures, and history of the district office. What he didn't prepare for, however, was the shift from working with others on an individual basis to dealing with people in a participatory, group situation. The new position required the use of team decision-making, peer review, staff negotiation, and group assessment.

The manager was aware of the emphasis on groups, but assumed his current management skills, which were well regarded, would see him through the change of focus. Trouble began within a few months. The manager's weekly meetings with his division supervisors generated more bickering and confusion than ideas and answers. Although he always provided a very structured agenda for the monthly meeting, the participants complained that their time was being wasted. Several of the group's members blamed the new director for a lack of leadership and an absence of a cohesive force.

In addition, his staff felt that he was insensitive to their suggestions and needs. They said he was too controlling and unwilling to take risks. The manager quickly found himself spending most of his time attending to problems. As soon as one crisis was resolved, two or three new issues would await his immediate attention.

"There was no mystery to his downfall," states Dr. Eicher. "The new director, although a good manager in many respects, had no awareness of how to run or use groups to his (or their) advantage. Going from one crisis to another was the result of his inability to recognize and respond to the personalities of the individual groups with which he worked."

Testing Your Group Awareness

Do you have the ability to recognize and respond to the groups with which you work? To assess the manager's level of group awareness, Dr. Eicher has developed a short quiz. Respond to each statement by checking the True or False column. Answers and explanations follow the quiz.

1. Team building is a direct result of the group leader's ability to motivate and inspire.

_____True   _____False

2. The most effective group leaders are those who exert control over their group.

_____True   _____False

3. Most groups go through similar stages of development.

_____True   _____False

4. Small groups (twelve members or fewer) are easier to work with than larger groups (thirteen members or more).

_____True   _____False

5. Participants who are more vocal tend to have more power.

_____True   _____False

6. Most groups, without the leader's influence, will solve their own problems and delegate their own tasks.

_____True   _____False

7. A group that experiences conflict tends to become more unified than a group without conflict.

_____True   _____False

8. The most effective method of dealing with a disruptive group member is for the leader to confront him or her directly.

_____True   _____False

9. Group rather than individual efforts tend to be more effective in solving problems.

_____True   _____False

10. The way a leader begins a group session is as important as how he or she ends it.

_____True   _____False

Answers and Explanations

Item 1.   False. Team building is a direct result of the ideas, thoughts, feelings, and experiences exchanged during the group's existence. The leader's ability to motivate and inspire may add to the group's experience, but it does not by itself generate team spirit. Keep in mind that team building involves a common or unifying force, a shared goal or objective. It takes the investment and commitment of the majority of the group members to achieve unity.

Item 2.   True. Effective group leaders do indeed exert control over their groups. Control typically involves setting the agenda, clarifying, facilitating, probing, questioning, monitoring, and, when necessary, intervening. Control is a function of the leader. When used appropriately, the group leader's control does not interfere with the free expression or spontaneity of the participants. Be careful not to confuse control with dominance.

Item 3.   True. Most groups do go through the same basic stages of development: fit, power, and support. During the first stage of development, fit, members question where they belong, what impact they'll have, and what roles they'll be expected to assume. In addition, they are usually concerned about how their behavior will be judged. Power, the second stage, involves control. Typical questions asked by members include: How much influence do I have? Who's really in charge? How is the delegation of tasks decided? Group members often criticize and challenge the leader. During the final stage of development, support, participants express positive feelings and listen attentively to one another as suggestions and resources are shared. Although all three stages apply to any group, they do not necessarily occur in order, nor do all groups reach the final stage, support. The more a leader is aware of these stages, the more effectively he or she can guide the group.

Item 4.   False. Generally, large groups (thirteen members or more) are as manageable as small groups (twelve members or fewer). In fact, large groups often generate more interaction, resources, and creative alternatives. Once a leader understands the stages of group development (fit, power, and support), the size of the group becomes less important. The group can reach a point at which it is too large to manage or monitor, however. The size of the group will vary according to the leader's skill and experience.

Item 5.   False. Vocal group members are not typically the power brokers in a group. It's often the quieter, more unassuming participants who have a strong influence on a meeting or discussion. Power does not depend on talking a lot; rather, it arises from timing, strategy, and impact. It's not uncommon for quieter members to speak up toward the end of a meeting or session. Their comments often carry significant weight simply because they haven't previously engaged in the discussion. Their remarks often shift the focus of the conversation or help the members reach an agreement or make a decision.

Item 6.   True. One of the interesting characteristics of groups is their ability to resolve their own problems and to delegate their own tasks. When an assigned or elected leader leaves the group for any reason, an initial period of confusion follows—the "fit" stage—but within a short time a new leader will emerge as the group begins to reshape itself. This phenomenon suggests that groups are far more resourceful and self-directed than observers once thought.

Item 7.   True. Conflict does tend to unify groups. Whether it occurs among individual members, between subgroups within the group, or between the leader and the participants, the key to achieving unity is to resolve the conflict. Once resolution has been accomplished, the conflict becomes part of the group's past experience. The sharing of a group past serves as a cohesive force. When participants are going through conflict, the leader's role is not necessarily to resolve it, but rather to facilitate the group's solution to the conflict.

Item 8. False. The most effective and productive way for a leader to cope with a disruptive participant is to let the group confront him or her directly. If, after a period of time, it becomes apparent that the group will not accept this responsibility, the leader may choose to intervene. The leader should keep in mind that the more responsibility participants are willing to assume for their own actions and reactions, the stronger and more cohesive the group will become.

Item 9. True. The combined efforts of a group are often more effective than those of individuals. There is one problem, though: group problem-solving is far more time-consuming. The group leader must remember that problem-solving is another way to build group unity. During this type of activity the leader should serve as a facilitator and resource person.

Item 10. False. Although starting and ending a group are both important activities, the first impressions will have a more profound impact—either good or bad—on members. A weak introduction can create feelings or expectations that may interfere with the group's development. A poor summary or incomplete closure, on the other hand, may cause some confusion or uncertainty but will not destroy the work accomplished during the meeting.

Evaluating Your Score

How well did you do? If you correctly answered eight or more items, Dr. Eicher thinks you have a very good understanding of the nature and function of groups. Accurately answering four to seven items indicates that you have an average understanding of group-development principles. Responding correctly to fewer than four items suggests that you need to improve your group awareness by reading, observing, and participating in group activities.

13

MOTIVATING
SPECIFIC EMPLOYEES

No manager can afford to ignore increasingly poor performance by a valued and experienced staff member. Yet as we mentioned earlier, it is not uncommon for capable and efficient subordinates slowly to wind down to a point where they are barely making a contribution. How do you motivate the failing subordinate? This kind of problem may go deep, and surface solutions will not take care of it. It will require time and attention. Here is what to look for in experienced workers:

- Are they going about their tasks without enthusiasm? For example, do they perform only the necessary tasks, appear to be coasting, and have their minds elsewhere?

- Are they easily distracted from work? Do they do nothing for stretches of time, handle outside business frequently, and often take long lunches?

- Are they dwelling on off-job problems? Do they talk about family problems, money problems, car trouble, or minor illnesses?

- Are they hostile or quick to anger? Do they abuse their subordinates for minor infractions?

- Are they becoming more private, no longer joining in with others, communicating more tersely, and becoming generally less alert, even absentminded?

Any of these characteristics, when accompanied by increasingly poor performance, is a fair indicator that employees are doing jobs that no longer bring them sufficient satisfaction or reward. These employees are experiencing frustration, their jobs having lost whatever promise they once held.

The problem is a serious one. You might achieve a short-term solution in any number of ways: making an unscheduled performance appraisal followed by sincere praise, having a heart-to-heart talk, prodding or cajoling, or awarding a salary increase. These will not bring long-term results, of course, because they do not deal with the problem.

To achieve lasting results with these workers, you as their superior must make it possible for the subordinates to motivate themselves anew. Right now they feel trapped by the "crippled career" syndrome. They feel they are making no progress toward the goals they once aimed for.

In order to rebuild these subordinates' enthusiasm, ask yourself one key question: What can I do to make these people like themselves better in their job? One of the most effective ways is to analyze the employees' situation by using a Job Subordinate Worksheet like the one in Exhibit 6 on the following page.

EXHIBIT 6

Job Subordinate Worksheet Form

1. Number of years in present job	1	3	5	7	9	More
2. How many people report to him or her?						
3. By what factor has responsibility increased?						
4. By what factor has work load expanded?						
5. How much interdepartmental contact does the job require?						
6. What is the frequency of reward/recognition in this job?						

ANALYZING A SUBORDINATE'S SITUATION

The Job Subordinate' Worksheet takes only a few minutes to fill in, but it requires honest decisions and hard thinking. Here is how to respond to the six points listed:

1. Circle the number of years the subordinate has been in his or her present job. If the number is four, for example, circle the line between 3 and 5.

2. Place an X in the spot that denotes the number of people reporting to this person. If the answer is "none," put an X on the line before 1.

The four points that follow will require decisions and hard thinking. For each of these points, use the printed numbers on top (years in job) to express degree.

3. *Increase in responsibility.* This is your assessment of how much the subordinate's job has grown in importance and broadened responsibilities. Put an X in the appropriate spot, using the following example as a rough guide:

1 = small increase in responsibility
5 = considerable increase
9 = great increase

4. *Work load expansion.* This is your assessment of the quantitative increase in work load over the years. This has nothing to do with increased responsibility, such as taking on tasks in other areas. It means more of the same kind of work. Suppose, for example, that a customer complaint manager, at time of hiring, took over a department that was processing 160 customer complaints a month. The manager's work load has doubled: the sheer weight of the job has increased, but the responsibility is the same. The job has been changing only in terms of quantity. Put an X in the appropriate spot, using the same rough guide as above to indicate work load expansion.

5. *Interdepartmental contact.* How much contact with others in the company—especially peer and higher level people—does this job require? Put an X in the appropriate spot, using this as a guide:

1 = very little contact required
5 = periodic contact
9 = frequent contact

6. *Reward and recognition.* With what frequency does the subordinate receive any form of recognition for achievement? One way to help you make this assessment is to turn the question around: Has the subordinate been taken for granted? Put an X in the appropriate spot:

1 = rarely
5 = from time to time
9 = fairly often

An Actual Case

Exhibit 7 is one manager's Job Subordinate Worksheet prepared for a highly regarded male subordinate:

1. The subordinate has been in the job seven years.

2. He has two people reporting to him.

3. His responsibility has increased considerably.

4. There has been a great increase in his work load.

5. He has very little contact with other departments.

6. He is infrequently recognized.

The manager's own assessment fingers the probable causes for this subordinate's drop in performance:

EXHIBIT 7

Job Subordinate Worksheet

	1	3	5	⑦	9	More
1. Number of years in present job	1	3	5	⑦	9	More
2. How many people report to him or her?	X					
3. By what factor has responsibility increased?			X			
4. By what factor has work load expanded?						X
5. How much interdepartmental contact does the job require?	X					
6. What is the frequency of reward/recognition in this job?				X		

- After seven years on the job, the subordinate still has only two people reporting to him.

- His work load has expanded enormously, but his area of responsibility has not.

- His contact with others in the company is almost zero. He deals almost exclusively with his two assistants and his boss.

- He has gone relatively unrecognized.

The seeds of the problem are plain to see in this manager's worksheet. Note that four of the X's are to the left of the circled 7 (years in the job). Ideally, these X's should be closer to the 7.

The more years a person spends in the same job, the more proof that person is likely to require from the boss and the company—over and above salary—that he or she is important to them. But this worksheet indicates that this employee, after seven years, probably feels less than important to his superiors.

Taking Necessary Action

Your best course is to take whatever action is possible, but some actions may not be applicable. For example, it may be impractical in some cases to provide for greater interdepartmental contact, although it can enrich a job.

But even a single action can begin to turn things around, raise the subordinate's self-esteem, and make him or her feel better.

Here are some things you can do for subordinates in similar situations:

• Broaden their planning responsibility. If a superior does all the planning, the subordinates may feel like robots no matter how well they perform. Let your subordinates share in planning their work.

• Let them set their own standards and objectives. They will be tougher on themselves while enjoying the work more, because they will be in charge. When subordinates are allowed to work this way, they feel that they are making progress toward a performance standard.

• Get your subordinates involved in problem-solving. Maybe the only problems they now solve are the emergencies. If so, let them know about other problems that may affect their area of responsibility, and ask them to start thinking about solutions.

• Let them widen their learning base. People can get bored with a job if there is nothing more for them to learn. In many instances, however, they have mastered only the technical aspects of their jobs. They may welcome some training in supervision, leadership, negotiation, or some other subject might add new dimension to the job.

• Ask for their ideas and opinions. Subordinates feel important if the boss consults them regularly. This is high recognition. It cannot be overdone if it is sincere.

• Increase their contacts with other people in the company. You can do this occasionally by delegating tasks that require your subordinates to deal with other managers or department heads. Dealing with higher level people can be challenging and can lend importance to the job.

• See to it that your subordinates have thinking time. If their work load is so enormous that they spend all their time just keeping up, they will have no time to prepare or to devise innovations. The job will become monotonous because they are always doing it and never thinking about it. They may need a chance to step back from their work and think about better, faster, or smarter ways to do it.

MOTIVATING THE PROFESSIONAL

Techniques for motivating scientific, technical, creative, and other professional specialists tend to be different—

sometimes very different—from those that motivate prod-uct-line supervisors. You will need to use different rewards and leadership techniques to get top performance and productivity from specialists in your organization. You may not have encountered this group yet in your management responsibilities. But eventually as you ascend that corporate ladder, you will. Here's some advice.

Virgil Whitney is a New York management consultant who specializes in development of management personnel. He has devised motivational programs for major companies like American Express and American Cork. He explained that differences in motivating line managers and staff specialists stem from the differences in the kinds of satisfaction they derive from their jobs.

A line manager, on one hand, tends to get psychological rewards from directing other people's efforts and from obtaining results through other people, rather than solely from personal efforts. The manager, in other words, may have a psychological need to exert power and influence. Such a manager is often impressed by symbols of power such as titles, luxurious offices, generous expense accounts, and a position on the company's organizational chart, and he or she may develop a strong identification with the company.

A staff specialist, on the other hand, whether in a scientific, technical, creative, or other professional field, tends to derive greater psychological reward from doing a particular job in which he or she can enjoy personal achievements and recognition for those achievements. The professional often develops as much or more personal identification with a professional field as with the company. Such a specialist wants to become known as an authority in the field and may get special satisfaction from the admiration of his or her peers in the speciality—a paper delivered at a professional meeting, for instance, or an article published in a professional journal.

Financial Remuneration

Whitney noted that line managers usually receive less recognition from their peers, so they're generally more concerned about salary. They tend to value themselves more for the money they earn than for their personal achievements on the job. Partly for this reason, many companies structure their reward systems to give the greatest financial rewards and symbols of power (such as titles, offices, and other perquisites) to line executives rather than to staff specialists.

But Whitney warns against the serious mistake of assuming that money isn't important to staff specialists. While large salaries may not significantly motivate them to perform better, they can become deeply dissatisfied and demotivated if they feel they are underpaid.

Many companies have serious morale problems because they refuse to reveal to employees how their salary systems work. Whitney emphasized that to avoid morale problems due to differences in pay among executives and professionals, a company needs a formal salary administration policy. It should make clear to all personnel that compensation for each job is based on such factors as accountability for the company's overall performance, technical knowledge, and responsibility for solving problems.

Professional Prestige

Even the fairest salary system won't result in top performance by a staff specialist, however, if the company ignores the specialist's psychological need for professional recognition. Helping such people win prestige within their profession can increase their loyalty to the company and spur them on to greater productivity. And it usually costs less money than a significant increase in salary. Whitney suggests three specific ways to recognize professional status:

1. Give professionals time off at full salary and pay their travel expenses to attend professional meetings. This will lead to renewed vigor for the job and may produce valuable new ideas for the company.

2. Pay for your professionals' membership in professional societies and encourage them to participate in their group's activities. This can also be a prestige builder for the company.

3. Pay for subscriptions to professional journals.

Each of these ways of recognizing a staff professional can more than pay for itself by improving job performance and raising productivity.

Whitney cited an example of a large company that specialized in manufacturing asphalt floor tiles. The company's research chemists felt creatively stifled by restrictions on the type of research they could do. They felt these restrictions prevented them from making a maximum contribution to the company by developing new products through basic research. They interpreted the restrictions as a sign that top management wasn't really interested in developing new products but merely wanted variations on the existing products.

When the company's management realized that a serious morale problem had developed among the chemists, the research and development operation was reorganized to provide for a reasonable amount of work on basic research. As a result, the chemists developed an entirely new type of floor tiles based on vinyl plastic instead of asphalt. This was a major breakthrough. It established the company as a leading manufacturer of an entirely new flooring product that has proven highly profitable.

MOTIVATING YOUR SECRETARY

You can profitably apply many standard techniques for motivation in your relationship with your secretary. But a special touch and extra sensitivity can really produce remarkable results in this critical alliance.

Here are some guidelines:

* Whether it's your secretary's first day or twentieth year on the job, you always treat him or her with respect. This is the single most important factor in motivating top performance and maximum productivity.

* Praise your secretary frequently, especially for a difficult job well done.

* Give constructive criticism when necessary, but avoid correcting more harshly than necessary. And never criticize your secretary publicly—*always* in private.

* Show personal interest without prying. For instance, occasionally ask about family or a personal problem.

* Take your secretary to lunch occasionally.

* Show consideration when you need overtime work. Let your secretary know as early in the day as possible. Never wait until five or ten minutes before the normal quitting time. Provide an opportunity to adjust any personal plans or commitments for the evening.

* Be considerate in adding to the work load. For instance, if your secretary hasn't been checking sales figures but now must take on that new duty, give as much advance notice as you can, and explain your reasons for expanding the work load.

- Offer more responsibility and authority as your secretary gains experience and ability. For example, give more control over correspondence. Invite your secretary to accompany you to important meetings and to represent you at routine meetings. This not only gives your secretary a psychological boost; it also saves you time.

- Keep your secretary advised of significant changes that lie ahead in your operation. Make sure you explain the reasons for them and how they will affect the job.

Job Enrichment

To keep their highly qualified secretaries, many executives are restructuring and expanding the jobs they do so that those jobs become more interesting and offer more challenge. Experienced and efficient secretaries want jobs in which brainpower is important. They don't want to sit at a typewriter all day. They want to function as a close assistant to the boss; they are eager to take some responsibility, authority, and power. They want to make decisions without having to get the boss's instructions or approval.

Methods of enriching secretarial jobs vary with each company and particularly with the personal style of each manager. The special abilities of each secretary are also an important factor, but here are some techniques that often prove effective:

Correspondence. If your secretary is capable of handling your correspondence, give him or her more and more control over it. Don't dictate every syllable of every letter. Let your secretary write routine letters and memos from scratch and sign such correspondence with his or her own name and the words "secretary to" over your name.

This can relieve you of much routine correspondence and give your secretary some professional satisfaction.

Telephone. Most secretaries screen incoming phone calls to spare their bosses from being pestered unnecessarily. But why not go further and let your secretary actually handle as many calls as possible for you, making whatever decisions are required?

Filing. Unless there's some overriding reason for not doing so, allow your secretary wide latitude over your filing system. After all, the person who must do the filing and retrieve material from the files should be allowed to adapt the system as much as possible to his or her own preferences and working methods. Some executives insist on controlling each detail of their filing systems, but this is usually a mistake. Your secretary's ideas on how to organize the files may be better than yours.

Job Title. After your secretary has become thoroughly experienced and proficient in the job and has acquired the ability to make effective decisions, consider changing that title from secretary to administrative assistant or executive assistant. Some companies routinely use this device to promote highly qualified secretaries. The new title increases their secretaries' prestige within the company and raises their self-esteem. Companies generally include an increase in salary with the title.

Purchasing. While many secretaries order stationery, pencils, and paper clips, it's not unusual for a company to buy more expensive office equipment without even consulting the secretaries who will use such equipment as typewriters, copying machines, automated telephone systems, or word processors. This can cause serious problems. For instance, secretaries know a great deal about typewriters and are likely to prefer one model over another. If you or your company should buy new typewriters without even consulting the secretaries, they may deeply resent your presumptuous action. The psychological effect may reduce their productivity.

PART III

The third segment of this book covers motivation from the viewpoint of managers on the firing line. It outlines case histories in which techniques have worked—and have failed.

You can read all the books on motivation that fill a library's shelves, and you can attend seminars and listen to speeches until you're an expert yourself. But the best way to learn how to motivate is to apply the practices you think will work in the reality of your workplace. That's what the managers quoted in the next few chapters have done.

Your company may not be as large as some of those cited; your employee population may be different; your current position may not offer you the opportunities that these managers had; and you may work in an entirely different economic environment. The point is that the shrewd manager learns from personal experience and especially from the experience of others, both successful and not so successful. So consider what these people did right and also what they did wrong.

If any techniques, suggestions, or tips are immediately applicable to your current situation, take advantage of them right now. If not, file them away for future reference as you move up in the corporate hierarchy at your firm. They may prove invaluable some time in the future.

THE CASE OF
THE MOTIVATED PRODUCTION
FACILITY: HEWLETT-PACKARD

Hewlett-Packard, Inc., is a worldwide manufacturer of sophisticated electronic products for industry, the medical profession, and the general public. It began operations in 1939 with an investment of less than $1,000. The founders, Dave Packard and Bill Hewlett, had been classmates at Stanford University.

They started the company with a clearly understood philosophy of management that was far ahead of its time. It remains today an outstanding example of a caring relationship between managers and workers, which motivates everyone involved. Hewlett-Packard (HP) has solved many of the problems of achieving motivational management. The concept and the actions that make it successful are known to both employees and managers as the HP Way. What is the HP Way? Bill Hewlett reported:

> It is the policies and actions that flow from the belief that men and women want to do a good job, a creative job, and

they will do so if they are provided with the proper environment. That's part of it. Coupled closely with this is the HP tradition of treating each individual with consideration and respect and recognizing personal achievements. Dave Packard and I honestly believe this and have tried to operate the company guided by this philosophy since we started.

HOW WORKERS DESCRIBE THE HP WAY

Employees at HP were asked to describe the HP Way. Here are a few representative comments:

- "It is a belief in people."
- "It is respect for the individual's self-esteem that is important."
- "It is recognition. A sense of achievement and importance."
- "It is security. A sense of permanence."
- "It is informality. A first-name basis for everyone."
- "It is performance and enthusiasm."

These comments were made anonymously as part of a regular survey by HP of employee attitudes. An examination of these comments reveals that each one results from the presence in HP of one or more of the motivating factors that behavioral scientists believe to be so vital to a motivating environment.

PROVIDING FOR WORKER SECURITY

"One of the earliest decisions Dave and I made when the company was formed," Hewlett explained, "is that we would not be a company that would seek large, lucrative contracts, employ a great many people during the life of the contract and, at its completion, let these people go. We sought to make our employees secure."

This policy has created a work force that is both experienced and loyal. Turnover of qualified people at HP is low, despite the intense competition from many other companies in the area for people with similar skills. Furthermore, while laws in some countries restrict companies' freedom to lay off workers or mandate that reduction in force be accomplished only with complete consultation and agreement with workers' representatives, HP management sought its own solution to making workers secure.

During the recession in 1970, orders fell, and HP faced large financial losses unless it reduced its labor costs by at least 10 percent. Although other companies in the same area fired their workers, HP rejected this approach. Tom Lowden, an executive in the personnel division, explained how:

> We decided we could save the money by reducing the work schedule from ten days to nine every two weeks by giving everyone a Friday off without pay. That included [everyone from] Hewlett and Packard down to the lowest-level employee. Everyone was delighted. In a few months, when orders picked up, we simply went back on full schedule without losing any members of the work force. Given HP's commitment to employee security, it was the only logical solution. A layoff would have been viewed as a betrayal of trust, and that would have been unforgivable.

THE VALUE OF TRUST

HP has demonstrated trust in other ways. Many years ago the company eliminated time clocks. They were unnecessary irritants in an atmosphere of trust; they wasted time and regimented workers.

HP also introduced the concept of flextime in most of its plants. Most employees may report to work at any time between six and eight in the morning. The only requirement is that they work an eight-hour shift. No one records who is reporting at what time. People are trusted. Lowden said,

> When you take out time clocks and introduce flextime you are telling people, "We trust you." If you put controls on who arrives at what hours, you are not trusting and everyone knows it. We know some people cheat. But they are a small minority, and you insult the majority when you punish everyone for the sins of a few. Most people do respond to a trusting relationship. It is management's lack of faith that causes the problems, not the workers taking advantage of trust.

This theme of trust will be repeated over and over in case histories focusing on motivation. Without it almost any motivational scheme is doomed to failure. With it, you can make up for almost any other motivational deficiency.

THE SUPERVISOR AND AUTONOMY

The major function of the HP supervisors is to solve problems. This is one of the first things the new employee learns. Throughout their employment, employees are constantly reminded that their supervisor is the source of all information, whether it be the location of a special tool or the amount of solder to use in a particular operation. Supervisors receive detailed instruction on all matters relating to the operation of HP and of their departments. In a rapid-growth, high-technology company there are frequent changes, so supervisors often attend refresher courses to acquaint them with the latest developments.

Said Lowden, "We expect our supervisors to answer almost any question without referring the questioner to anyone higher up. We expect them to apply common sense to answering questions relating to personal problems. And we expect them to direct questioners to professional sources if they have any doubts about their own competence to deal with the problem."

Problem-solving supervisors must have authority to do what they think necessary. For example, an employee in one department devised a faster way to perform multiple soldering operations on an electronic oscillator. She discussed the idea in detail with her supervisor. Implementing it would cost money, however, and require retraining all those working on that instrument. In many companies the supervisor at this point would have called in the department manager, who might then have called in another boss, and weeks or months would have gone by. But not at HP. The supervisor decided the idea should be implemented at once. His authority allowed him to make the expenditures needed and hold up production long enough to train the employees in the new method. He told his own manager of the decision as a matter of courtesy and information, and was congratulated for his initiative. The woman who suggested the idea was complimented, and her story and picture were featured in the company newsletter.

This example illustrates several motivational factors that are inherent in the HP Way. The supervisor's role as a problem-solver allowed the employee freedom to innovate. Because the supervisor had authority and autonomy, he could provide the employee with immediate acceptance of her idea. Because of the supervisor's role, the employee felt that she had a voice in how the work could be done. The supervisor was a good listener, one of the most important aspects of good supervision. His willingness to listen, as well as the company's policy of having him act as a problem-solver showed that the company cared about an employee's idea enough to invest considerable money and time in it.

This may be a good point at which to think about the supervisors who report to you or who report to the management position that you'd eventually like to attain. What are their roles? How much authority and autonomy do they have? Are they good listeners? Are they effective problem-solvers? Remember that the better you make your staff, the better you'll look in the end.

REWARDS AND INCENTIVES

HP uses an informal system of rewards for outstanding work. Lowden explained this system:

> A person has worked extra hard on some task. The department manager, usually alerted by the supervisor, takes the person aside and says, "You did an excellent job, and I appreciate your efforts, and so does the company. Please take this $100 and do whatever you want with it. Enjoy yourself. You've earned it." Then the manager notifies the editor of the company paper who may do a write-up on that employee. It's simple and uncomplicated.

HP offers sabbatical leaves as another way to reward excellence. They can be granted by the department head.

Leave may be requested by the employee or suggested by a manager. "Sabbatical leave is a reward, not only for real, measurable accomplishments but also for leadership, co-operation, and just plain hard work," Lowden said. "We don't care how the individual spends that leave. Some people go to school. Some travel for pleasure, and some visit other production facilities. HP feels that whatever people learn on sabbatical leave may someday be of value to them or the company."

HP also introduced a profit-sharing program that distributed money to over thirty thousand employees. The company emphasized the importance of cost reduction, quality, and volume of production. It tried to impress each employee with the importance of profit for the successful achievement of the company's objectives.

In many countries profit-sharing is a mandatory business practice, but HP's plan was voluntary. It helped convince even the lowest-level worker that an effort to increase profit would result in personal reward. Company executives, however, do not regard profit-sharing as a motivational factor; they see it as a logical and just reward for employees whose work exceeds in quality and quantity similar work done by competitors. Profit-sharing is not a giveaway program. HP believes that workers are entitled to share in the benefits that accrue from their efforts.

CONTINUOUS TRAINING

The supervisors at HP work closely with individuals called lead persons. These are highly skilled individuals who provide technical guidance at the worksite. If a supervisor notices that a worker is having difficulty accomplishing a task because of faulty technique, the lead person is called in to provide intensive, one-on-one training. The supervisor does not sit down with the employee or get involved in the work. To do so would interfere with the supervisor's real job.

In this way HP provides continuous training of the most useful type, since it occurs when needed. The company does have many regular, formal training programs, but the supplementary lead person is another addition to the motivational climate in this company.

HP discovered that rapid expansion resulted in lead persons performing supervisory functions in addition to their technical jobs. The HP Way rewards people in accordance with what they do, and so lead persons who were performing many supervisory functions were promoted to supervisors. Others were promoted to the position of lead person. Thus, recognition was given for performance, and opportunities for advancement were obvious to workers, lead persons, and supervisors.

MANAGEMENT BY WANDERING AROUND (MBWA)

Managers at HP engage in an unusual management style that they call Management by Wandering Around (MBWA). This concept is based on the belief that significant activities occur at the place where the work is done and not necessarily in the confines of a manager's office. Lowden explained it this way:

> We tell our managers to go to the shop floor and communicate face-to-face. Find out what is really going on. We don't write memos when we can go see each other. We don't like the telephone for internal communication. It puts a barrier between people. At any time of the day or night you will find HP managers, including Hewlett and Packard, talking to anyone about anything, and listening. Mostly listening. We listen

more than we talk because we think that is the best way to learn.

MBWA implies that office doors are always open and that no one makes an appointment to see someone else. Managers at HP do not have the luxurious high-status offices that exist in many corporations. All offices are about the same. It is difficult to tell the office of the production manager from the office occupied by several secretaries.

Offices are arranged on the open layout, with small cubicles scattered around a large open room. There is a lot of glass, so that manager A, wanting to discuss something with manager B, simply looks over to see if B is in his or her space and walks over to talk. Combine this sytem with the practice of calling all employees by their first names and the company develops an informal atmosphere. This characterizes the relationships among peers and between superior and subordinate. All workers are motivated to achieve the objectives of the company at least partly because of the ease of communications and the opportunity for immediate feedback.

There are no suggestion boxes anywhere within HP. Management believes that requiring workers to submit written notes will discourage them from making suggestions. Workers with ideas simply tell them to the nearest supervisor or to the first manager they see walking around. Every worker is assured of an attentive listener and a prompt, carefully considered response. If the idea can be used, the individual making the suggestion will receive recognition.

FREEDOM TO PLAN WORK

Division managers have wide latitude to operate their departments. Top management establishes objectives with division managers and leaves them free to work toward accomplishing them. Since managers are products of the HP Way, they never resort to policies that run counter to the HP principle. When managers are innovative, the headquarters staff will study what is being done at the division level to see if it can be profitably applied to the whole company. As Lowden explained,

> We do not want to become too involved in how managers get their jobs done, as long as they don't violate the HP Way. The method is relatively unimportant as long as the desired quality is built into the final product. We know that [all employees do] their own jobs better if they have freedom to be innovative about details and procedures. This applies equally to managers and workers. We look at every idea with an open mind. What is important is creating an atmosphere where people aren't afraid to make suggestions.

PHYSICAL ENVIRONMENT

A trip through the headquarters administrative area shows another side of the HP Way. The company allows individuals to personalize the decor of their offices. The result is that a sterile office environment is transformed into a homelike atmosphere. No restrictions are placed on the display of personal photographs or art objects on desks or shelves. Management requires only that decor or art objects not offend others, not interfere with work, and not constitute a safety hazard. There are no nameplates on desks or cubicles. At HP all employees know the name and location of their supervisor. Nameplates would be superfluous.

"Our people know what their tasks are, and they do them without a supervisor constantly checking them," Lowden said. "We help one another. When the work we have to do is finished, we know where it goes, and we are free to take it there. We may assist one another, exchange work or take a break without discussing the matter with anyone. We are trusted to do what is right. Supervisors don't keep track of the comings and goings of the workers. They do know what is accomplished. They do concentrate on the even allocation of work and the important function of training."

HP has not solved the problem of the boring job, but it has reduced the stultifying effect such dead-end jobs have on workers. Its solution is to select the right person for the job. In Lowden's words,

We know we can't make every job exciting and challenging. We also know that some individuals are content to perform repetitive tasks. Therefore we spend a great deal of effort interviewing to select people for boring jobs who will be least likely to become dissatisfied. We also find it helpful to rotate people from one relatively simple, repetitive job to another similar job. By so doing we extend the time a person can work at a boring job without becoming ineffective. Perhaps the most constructive thing this does for workers is to demonstrate our respect for them.

This type of familiarity and lack of a caste system has its negative aspects also. If it is not an integral part of the philosophy of the company as a whole, it can breed bad habits and lack of discipline. If your entire division or company isn't run on this premise, be careful about attempting to incorporate it into your domain only. Remember, that dream of yours to reach the executive suite *does* include the fancy gold lettering on the oak door to your corner suite of offices.

MOTIVATION THROUGH GOAL-SETTING

HP also got involved in a long-term project designed to bring the technique of Management by Objectives (MBO) down to the level of the average workers. The aim was to design an MBO program that would allow relatively un-skilled persons to decide how to proceed with a task. Man-agers would explain to the workers what end results they expected. Then they would ask the workers how to achieve those ends.

The workers would select their own tools and methods and their own standards. By making such a program a re-ality, HP calculated that it could change the attitudes of a large number of unskilled workers by giving them, for the first time, real control over what they did and how they did it.

A copy of HP's proposed plan to bring MBO down to the clerical level appears as Exhibit 8. MBO has been suc-cessfully applied to all levels of management and supervi-sion at many companies, although it is not as popular today as it once was. It is not at all common at low-employee levels. The concept does contain many of the motivational factors considered important by the theorists. They include increasing job satisfaction by broadening tasks and increas-ing responsibility; some freedom to plan work; a voice in how work is to be done; potential for feedback on perfor-mance from clients; trust; training.

EXHIBIT 8

HP's Plan for MBO at the Clerical Level

A PLAN FOR IMPLEMENTING MBO AT THE CLERICAL LEVEL AT HP

MAJOR RESPONSIBILITIES.
What must be done?

PERFORMANCE STANDARDS.
How well must it be done? (desired results)

EXAMPLE: POSITION PLANNING FOR A SUPPORT JOB.
Purpose—to assist in the development of sales-region personnel by providing:

Product/Service	clerical/administrative support
Customer/Client	to the sales-region development group
Scope	in the Corporate Training Department

MAJOR RESPONSIBILITIES	MEASURES OF PERFORMANCE
Producing draft and final typed copies of course materials, overheads, etc.	Promptness and accuracy, good layout, grammar and punctuation corrections
Handling correspondence, mail, expense reports	Same as above plus prompt out-basket servicing, mail screened and rerouted
Handling telephones and inquiries	Knowledgeable enough to answer inquiries and provide information about department activities and resources

MAJOR RESPONSIBILITIES	**MEASURES OF PERFORMANCE**
Administrative assistance, including logistics and materials production for pilot programs, expense tracking, etc.	Accuracy, completeness, planning ahead
Departmental backup (assisting other secretaries in telephone and clerical backup)	Answer before second ring, customer relations standards, share typing peak loads
Checking out library books; maintaining cabinets, bookcases	Keep department area neat, discard junk

HP's performance evaluation forms are designed around Position Planning. If you and your manager have not had an opportunity to develop a Position Plan, you will want to get started on it prior to your next evaluation.

CARING AS A MOTIVATIONAL FORCE

Barbara Johnstone held a unique position at HP. Her function was to serve as an adviser to anyone with a problem. She was located in the center of the production area where she was readily accessible at any time to everyone. Most important, she worked at being a good listener.

"All kinds of problems occur, ranging from family difficulties to insurance complications to personality clashes," she explained. "My goal is to get help as soon as possible, take people's minds off their personal problems so they can work and not worry." Providing workers with a person with this function is a measure of HP's concern for its employees.

Caroline Hendrickson, a sheet-metal worker, came to HP in 1971 with limited industrial experience. She worked first as a cable layer, transferred to soldering, and then moved to sheet metal. "I asked my foreman if I could try a better job," she said. "He always said, 'Try it! If you can't succeed, come back here. You do well with us.' To me, that's part of the spirit around here. If you want to try another job everyone is happy to help you. You can go as far as you want, and HP will back you all the way." Opportunities for advancement or development in the present job are always open at HP. Few if any workers think their path to a better job is blocked.

HP's managerial style might be described as selfishly altruistic, a contradiction in terms but a reasonable description of the system. Management believes that the selfish objective of high profit is best achieved by adopting an altruistic attitude toward the welfare of the work force.

The system has worked for HP for many years, not only in Palo Alto, California, and many other cities in the United States, but also in Europe and Asia where HP has plants and administrative and sales offices. Workers in Singapore and France, in Japan and Germany, in Canada and Puerto Rico participate in the same programs and benefit from the same managerial philosophy. Apparently concepts of the HP Way cross social and cultural barriers without losing their validity or attractiveness.

THE CASE OF
THE MOTIVATED OFFICE:
OCCIDENTAL INSURANCE

The Occidental Insurance Company, headquartered in Los Angeles, was founded more than seventy years ago and is one of the largest insurance companies in the world. The problems of motivation that Occidental faces are similar to those found in any clerical operation where large volumes of paper must be handled efficiently and where numerous customer inquiries must be promptly answered.

Office work below the managerial level suffers from a poor image. The word "clerk" evokes no feelings of pride. Many people accept clerical jobs because they lack skills or as an easy way to supplement a family income. To further complicate the problems of providing a motivating environment, few large offices hold out hope of promotion to clerks. Until recently clerks have seen themselves trapped in dead-end jobs that were uninteresting and poorly paid. Supervisors concentrated on job details and paid little attention to human needs. Clerks felt unappreciated and knew they had little choice concerning how they would perform their jobs.

The working environment for most clerical employees is depressing. Offices are often contain endless rows of gray metal desks lined up with military precision. Supervisors are usually located where they can watch everything. Clerks are expected to stay at their desks.

RISING CLERICAL COSTS
FORCE CHANGES

Cost analysis showed that in the late Seventies, in Occidental's office, a letter responding to a customer's inquiry cost as much as seven dollars if it was done correctly the first time. A badly written or poorly typed letter, or one that contained misinformation, had to be done over, and the costs escalated. Thus Occidental saw the need for improvement. Turnover of clerical personnel was running at a rate considerably higher than those of other companies with similar operations. Morale was low.

Company officials knew that change was essential and would take time. They realized that they must develop an organization that would integrate individual goals at every level of employment with corporate objectives. They also foresaw many problems. Introducing a new and innovative style of managing and of work would be fraught with risks. Managers and supervisors, accustomed to old ways, would resist change. Employees might view the changes as just another way to get more work out of them.

As you attempt to incorporate the suggestions of this book into your management style, you might face similar resistance. Don't let it discourage you. Eventually your new motivation skills will pay off.

THE ASSUMPTION OF THEORY Y

Richard Durkee, Occidental's second vice-president in charge of personnel and organizational development at the time, was selected to manage the creation and introduction of changes that would create a motivated work force. The Occidental effort assumed that McGregor's Theory Y was essentially correct. "Trust is crucial," Durkee declared. "We believe that people will respond in a mature manner to management's efforts to make the job more attractive. We have found that they do respond when trusted. Our biggest problem is convincing lower-level managers and supervisors of the value of developing a trusting relationship."

DEVELOPING MOTIVATION FROM TOP LEVELS OF MANAGEMENT DOWN

In 1972 Occidental introduced Management by Objectives. It was recognized that this step would have little impact on the clerical staff. But the company believed that MBO offered the best system to introduce the concepts of individual goal-setting and individual responsibility for results. Once managers and supervisors understood how MBO worked for them, they would be better able to appreciate the value of goals for their subordinates and to understand their own responsibilities for helping subordinates achieve. Durkee explained:

> We saw MBO as a beginning, but we quickly realized that it would not have any immediate effect on clerical workers. There was an urgent problem at the lowest clerical level and we needed an immediate response. We decided to introduce

early closing on Fridays. We would ask each person to work only five and a half hours on Friday, for full pay. We could not afford to lose the work that would normally be done on that day. So we agreed that time lost on Friday would not be made up on any other day but employees would do their utmost to accomplish in five and half hours the same amount of work they usually produced in eight. That's the way we introduced the idea.

In effect, clerical workers now had a specific goal.

Initially, some employees resented the idea. They had difficulty understanding that they were actually receiving pay for two and a half hours when they were not at work and that being asked to work harder was not an imposition but a fair exchange. Overall, however, the idea was well accepted. After several months supervisors reported that Friday production was equal to that of other days. People just worked faster on Friday and exceeded standards.

MORE CLERICAL-LEVEL CHANGES

Durkee said, "I think that clerical workers looked forward to the short workday on Friday and made up their minds to work very hard. Because they had a goal they could reach and the reward—the free time—was worth the effort, the work got done, and no one felt overworked."

After the short day on Friday became accepted, the company made its next change for the benefit of the clerical force. It established flextime, in the same manner as Hewlett-Packard and with essentially the same results. There were really heated objections in the beginning at Occidental, however, something that did not occur at HP.

"Many managers and supervisors predicted wholesale violations," Durkee recalled. "Some objected so strenuously to the concept that we had to make it clear we were ordering flextime into effect. It was a very difficult time for management. If our chief executive had not been strongly committed to this improvement, those of us who were trying to introduce the concept would have been overwhelmed by the objectors."

But, as it had at HP, flextime worked well—another indication that trust and caring are necessary for an internally motivated work force. Occidental also eliminated time clocks, reasoning that if people are to be trusted they must be trusted all the way; there is no such thing as half trusting.

GOAL-SETTING FOR CLERICAL EMPLOYEES

By the mid-seventies managers accepted the MBO concept. Durkee decided to adapt the concept to the level of the clerical employee by introducing a program of goal-setting. This differed from pure MBO in at least two ways.

First, the goals were dictated by the nature of the work to be done. For instance, a clerk who prepared an insurance policy had little discretion about what to include. Therefore, a goal must be strictly a matter of quality and quantity, with little opportunity for innovation.

Second, broad goals, such as "accomplishing my assigned work in half the time" were not feasible. Such a goal might have been appropriate for a supervisor with multiple responsibilities when applied to one facet of the job. For a clerk, whose major responsibility involved only the preparation of a form or the typing of a variety of letters, the goal of doing it in half the time would simply invite errors.

"What we were trying to accomplish was to give our clerks individual responsibility for their own portion of the work," Durkee said. "Once clerical workers understood how to set reasonable goals for themselves and then reach or exceed them, we figured we had laid the foundation on which we could later build an expanded program of setting goals and taking on greater responsibilities."

The idea introduced them to the relationship between supervisor and worker that leads to real cooperation. Clerks learn what their supervisor considers a job well done. Supervisors learn what the clerks believe they can do within a specified time. Durkee described the results:

> We found that the new young managers were much more trusting. They were willing to allow people freedom to control their own activities and did not feel threatened by the most innovative suggestions. Their typical reaction was, "That's interesting. Let's try it." The newer managers seemed to understand the MBO concept better than some older ones. After we introduced MBO, we found that change is deeply disturbing to some people. MBO shifts power from the authoritarian individual to a participative management style, and this is a frightening change. The young managers had learned about MBO in theory at school, and they were eager to put it into practice.

One question must always be asked about MBO: Management by *whose* objectives? If the answer is "By the managers' objectives to the exclusion of any suggestions by the employees," the program will fail. Any changes made to improve the motivating environment will cause some reaction among employees elsewhere in a company. Ramifications of changes must be carefully thought through before being implemented.

Whether or not your company has a formal MBO program in place, you should know some of the pros and cons of MBO from a motivational standpoint. And your knowledge shouldn't be based on textbook theory alone. That's why other managers' experience with MBO will be very instructive.

DO'S AND DON'TS OF MBO

Based on managers' experiences, here are some things to do and not to do to achieve and maintain an effective MBO system:

- *Do* establish credibility for Management by Objectives throughout your organization by insisting on top management participation and backing no matter what level MBO is being installed at.

- *Do* plan carefully to get the program started. Be sure adequate provisions are made for educating managers and other employee groups on the basics.

- *Do* allow adequate time for Management by Objectives to take hold; years of doing things a certain way cannot be reversed overnight.

- *Do* develop measurable objectives; everyone—including you—must be able to determine when the results have been achieved.

- *Do* tie Management by Objectives into existing information and control systems; changes in the systems can be made as more experience is gained and management's needs for information change.

- *Do* reward good performance; managers and workers alike should be able to relate results to rewards.

- *Do* stimulate discussion about MBO at all company levels, particularly during the implementation phase.

- *Do* review progress periodically and provide for information dispersal.

- *Don't* overemphasize objectives. Individual objectives are the heart of MBO, but they are only a part of the job. Objectives change. Not all will be achieved if they are truly challenging. Too many variables are involved, and some are beyond the control of the individual.

- *Don't* generate a "system" built on paper and emphasize the system rather than results.

- *Don't* allow favorite projects as objectives or accept routine, trivial objectives.

- *Don't* insist on an inflexible program or process; Management by Objectives should change as conditions require.

- *Don't* use MBO as the means to discipline or criticize employees' performance.

- *Don't* expect Management by Objectives to solve all management's problems.

SOCIAL RESPONSIBILITY
AS MOTIVATION

Occidental realized that its efforts to improve morale within the office would be slow to develop. Durkee knew that he should not try to introduce too many work-connected programs all at once. The company thought that there were other things it could do to raise morale and generate interest, however.

Durkee recalled that Peter Drucker insisted that the corporation has a responsibility for the welfare of the society in which it operates and which provides it with its work force. From this thought was born the Involvement Corps, a voluntary employee organization dedicated to improving the quality of life in the inner city of Los Angeles where Occidental was headquartered. The Involvement Corps attracted some five hundred employees who worked closely with the social service organizations serving the inner city. They performed tasks such as typing, filing, and advising on the preparation of forms. They also offered assistance in fields where they had personal expertise. In Durkee's words:

> We draw many of our employees from outside the city itself. At night, the majority of them travel into the suburbs, leaving behind the inner city and its problems. Many of them perform volunteer social services in their own communities, and we support those activities, but as a company we really belong to the inner city. We thought that our employees would be willing to divide their efforts between their home communities and the inner city if we encouraged such action and provided time to do useful volunteer work. This had little to do with the operation of an office, but it affected morale. We have found that when people are involved in a worthwhile activity and are supported by their employer, they develop a closer rapport with that employer. They ask their supervisors and managers for assistance in their volunteer activities and the cooperative attitude that develops spills over into job-related work in the office. This enhances the trusting relationship. We must have the trust of these employees as we move ahead with our long-range programs to improve the quality of office work.

Pressures build up among workers in an office. Durkee concluded that the company ought to provide an outlet through which employees could vent their dissatisfactions, ideas, and comments concerning anything not directly related to their work. Since there was already an active suggestion program for job-connected ideas, this new program, called Rap Up, was aimed at such problem areas as the cafeteria, transportation, personal problems, and just plain gripes. Durkee explained it this way:

> Herzberg calls these things hygiene factors and suggests that management should not worry about them. We disagree. While it is true that management cannot satisfy everyone who has a complaint, we can demonstrate our concern and our willingness to respond. We pay attention to what we learn through Rap Up, and we make some changes promptly. It often matters little what management does as long as it does something. Any action indicates that we are listening. No action tells everyone we don't care, and that is the worst impression to create.

ASSUMPTION OF RESPONSIBILITY

At first, office workers are likely to be reluctant to assume more responsibility. But with patience and good instruction from their supervisors, they improve. With the assumption of responsibility for results comes pride in performance. That's essential in motivating the worker. The most effective steps you can take to motivate workers will be those that give individuals some control over what they do and how they do it. You can't remove the routine from all office jobs, but you can allow individuals to exercise their judgment and initiative.

Your first tasks are (1) to develop responsibility in your clerical people and (2) to provide training that will open a career path for entry-level clerks. The key to success lies in the ability to develop workers who are interested in their work, who want to produce good work, and who are encouraged to do so by managers and supervisors who care about people and their accomplishments.

You can improve some routine office jobs by allowing people some freedom of choice on how to get the job done. If you tell your workers to drive nails in a board all day, it won't be long before the sheer drudgery of the job wears them down. Your best move is to give them a choice of where to drive the nail. Encourage them to experiment with the rhythm of their actions. Compliment them on their accomplishments. Show them there is some useful purpose for what they are doing. This will make the job more tolerable for a time.

MAKE CHANGES GRADUALLY

"You could create total chaos by introducing wholesale changes in procedure," Durkee declared. He went on to explain:

> We make changes one at a time, then see what reaction results. Sometimes a change creates more problems than it eliminates. That's discouraging for those who are committed to making the office a better place to work. You have to believe that improvement is possible. We have seen enough changes in attitude during the years we have been trying to improve the quality of office working life to believe we're moving in the right direction. But it is hard to develop measurable results. This is the most frustrating part of the effort. Our critics demand proof that our efforts do, in fact, motivate and we cannot always provide them. We do survey attitudes and compare what appears to be the situation today with what it appeared to be some years ago.

Occidental reported that turnover of clerical personnel was reduced to about half of what it had been when the programs began. Absenteeism also decreased, and morale, while largely unmeasurable, appeared to improve. While Durkee didn't want to lay complete credit at the door of these programs, he is convinced the efforts were worthwhile.

16

THE CASE OF
ORGANIZATION FOR
THE MOTIVATION:
KAISER PERMANENTE

By the late seventies, the Kaiser Permanente Medical Care Program served about 1.5 million people who paid a monthly fee that entitled them to health care services. Kaiser Permanente moved motivational theory out of the classroom into the work environment. It formed a department of organization research and development directed by Bernard Estafen. The department was responsible for developing "self-renewing, self-correcting systems of people who learn to organize themselves in a variety of ways, according to the nature of their individual tasks and who continue to cope with the rapidly changing demands the environment makes on the organization." Estafen said,

> We are convinced that those who actually do the work are in the best position to understand what should be done and how it should be done. The managers must depend on the

workers to tell them how to make a process get results more efficiently. The farther away the boss is from the activity of the workplace, the less understood are the details of the work and the less obvious are the real obstacles that hinder good performance.

The boss will always know some things better than the worker. In rare instances the boss may have a complete understanding of everything the worker does. In this circumstance the boss can make good decisions about the actual job requirements. For example, the medical professional who performs an operation certainly knows more about surgical technique than even the most competent assistant. But when that same surgeon tries to supervise the internal operations of a department—the office routine, its arrangement and the relationship of the department to others—the understanding is lower than with the people who do the work. Those decisions on work will often be defective.

Since the professional cannot tell the workers the best way to do their jobs, he or she must provide a means by which the workers can identify what needs to be done and do it. That's where my organization comes into the picture. We are the facilitators who make possible open communication from the group to the boss so that real problems are identified, real obstacles attacked, and practical solutions provided.

Estafen and his department served as internal consultants for the company, but they had no authority to impose solutions. Because they never give orders, they are not a threat to the head of any department that uses their services. Because they never impose solutions, individual workers don't feel that their working life has been governed by an outsider. Thus, the organization research and development department gets full cooperation from the groups it works with. Here is how a typical situation develops.

RECOGNITION OF PROBLEMS

Usually a problem becomes evident when one or more of the following conditions occurs: falling productivity, increasing complaints, higher turnover, complaints about or clashes between departments. Estafen is then asked to come in and identify the problem. He explained the procedures he follows:

> The first order of business is to identify the real problem. I accompish this by giving a questionnaire of some 140 questions to the members of the group being examined. These questions are developed to fit particular types of work. Questions intended for a group in a medical office would be different from those developed for a group working in a steel foundry. The thrust of them is "What's important to you about your job?" They seek to uncover both positive and negative aspects of the work.
>
> We work with groups, not individuals. Certainly the individual is important and will benefit from what we accomplish. But it is the group that gets the job done. When the group is satisfied, the work situation improves.

After the employees complete the questionnaire, Estafen tabulates their answers to each question and then conducts a "feedback session" with a group of about ten persons, including the boss. Estafen tells the group, "So many of you said this about this question." Then, as he describes the answers, the group decides which of them represent problem areas. Estafen does not indicate at any time what he considers important.

"The group considers all the answers. Normally it will conclude, after some discussion, that many of the problems identified are inconsequential and can be ignored," Estafen explained. "From the discussion we identify ten or fifteen urgent problems that are worthy of further attention. These are the targets we want to take care of."

GROUP CONSIDERATION
OF PROBLEMS

Estafen writes these problems on a large pad of paper before the group. He makes sure that his phrasing represents what the group intends to say. If there is disagreement, he clarifies the wording until all agree with it. Then the group begins to formulate action suggestions that will eliminate the problem.

"We find that about 90 percent of the problems can be changed by action within the group itself. The remaining 10 percent will need action by higher authority," Estafen said. "Our function then is to develop group solutions for the 90 percent. The organization research and development department does not make suggestions or give orders. We keep the discussion moving so that everyone in the group feels free to contribute ideas. It is the group that makes things happen."

The problems that cannot be resolved by the group are presented in a joint session between the group and representatives of the next higher management level. There are certain rules for this presentation: the higher-level managers agree that they will listen only; there will be no arguments, no sarcastic comments, no absolute yes or no responses during the meeting. Later, the higher-level representatives will meet to decide what they will do about the problems.

Their response may be "No, we cannot do that." The group can accept that response because it has had a fair hearing and has had an explanation that a solution, for the present, is impossible. What is not acceptable is no response at all. Higher levels must always respond one way or another to group suggestions.

WHY THIS MOTIVATIONAL TECHNIQUE GETS RESULTS

What are the results of this exercise? Estafen said they are astonishing:

> In the first place, the group owns the problem and the solution. The group identified it, discussed it, provided a solution for it. People will work hard to make their ideas work well. Because it was a group solution, no individuals feel ignored or left out of the discussion. There has been compromise and cooperation. The group has received recognition from higher authority and been complimented for its efforts. Recognition for excellent work is a very powerful device and further enhances the feelings of self-worth already created by the efforts of the group members in their own behalf.
>
> The organization research and development people have imposed no solutions. The group has been given absolute authority to control its own activities as they affect each individual in the group and its relations with other groups. The members of the group control their working life, and every sound theory of motivation insists that this is the critical ingredient for success.

Kaiser Permanente's top management recognized a fact in human relations that other managers often overlook, the fact that power blocks the free flow of information. Many times, managers hear only what their subordinates want them to hear—things that reflect credit on them and won't cause a change in the status quo.

This is often an unconscious defensive reaction by subordinates. They have learned that it is unwise to tell the boss the entire truth. They believe that sometimes their superiors want to hear only good news. As a result, negative facts are constantly screened out as information goes upward so that the person at the top never suspects trouble. This is a human tendency. You can combat it by holding frequent feedback sessions between the different levels of organization so that the real facts pass upward without censorship. It is the best way for the top boss to keep in touch with reality.

This is especially important to remember as you assume more responsibility and power at your company. An open-door policy does you no good if the only people who come through it are yes-men and yes-women. Sometimes the old story about killing the messenger who bears bad news can hit very close to home. Make sure you're not the one who performs the execution.

MEASURING THE EFFECTS OF MOTIVATION

Unlike other motivational techniques, this one produced measurable results at Kaiser. Estafen can use production figures from before and after his organization did its job to point out real improvements.

"It may be the number of patients cared for by the group or papers handled or medical prescriptions dispensed," Estafen said. "Whatever the group does, it can be measured before and after. There are always definite, measurable improvements, provided the facilitator has kept opinions out of the discussions and the group has developed its own solutions."

Certain jobs cannot be subjected to the group solution. Highly technical jobs performed by experts, for example, are not affected by group dynamics. Estafen is aware of this fact:

> We recognize two types of problems. There is the expert problem, where there is a recognized authority whose word is taken without argument, as for example, a brain surgeon. No one who is not a brain surgeon would presume to tell one how to operate. The other type is a process problem. Here there is no expert, but a group engaged in a process of some kind. When the expert has a problem, we step in only to facilitate the search for a solution. The group we call together to work on the problem is made up of other professionals who, though they may not understand the particulars of the problem, have empathy with their professional colleague and help with suggestions. Expert problems are a minority but when they arise they call for prompt action since they can have serious consequences.

The help of an organization such as the one Estafen manages is expensive, but there are consultants who perform similar functions. Most companies can afford their services.

"Kaiser Permanente needs to have our kind of organization at its command," Estafen said. "We make the difference between a company that does enough to get by and one that seeks and delivers excellence. We motivate because we stimulate people to devise their own solutions to problems. They have then created something. They cannot permit it to fail because if it does, they have failed themselves."

At the basis of many of the motivation procedures you attempt will be this concept: if you can convince people that something is their idea or brainchild—that they hold the success or failure of the job, project, or action in their hands—then you will have motivated workers.

17

A CASE OF A NEW METHOD OF MOTIVATION: QUALITY CIRCLES

A comparatively recent development in applying motivational theories to industrial plants is the quality circle. This concept originated in Japan in 1962 ana now involves over eight million workers throughout that nation.

The quality circle was introduced in the United States in 1974 through the efforts of Donald Dewar, an industrial engineer who became discouraged with scientific management concepts. Dewar went to Japan to study the quality circle program. After returning to the United States, he established the International Association of Quality Circles. The program has been introduced into many U.S. companies, including International Harvester, Boeing, General Motors, Sperry Vickers, and Westinghouse.

The quality circle consists of a small group of employees in the same work area who have been trained to identify and analyze problems related to their own jobs. When they have completed an analysis of a problem and devised a solution to it, they formally present the solution to management. Dewar had this to say about the program:

> We believe that the workers are the real experts in the work they do. Industrial engineers think they understand job-related problems, but they do not. I was one for many years, and I seldom got down to the level of the person on the machine. If workers are trained to recognize and solve problems they will find better ways to do the work.
>
> The circles are real motivators. Nothing makes most people more interested and excited about their work than the power to decide how it shall be done. Workers, often for the first time, find themselves talking with top management about real problems.
>
> They discover that they know how the work can best be done, and often they are able to convince management to change procedures. It's a tremendous boost for morale and gives the workers a great sense of pride.

QUALITY CIRCLES
AT SPERRY VICKERS

The Sperry Vickers Division of Sperry Rand, Inc., in Jackson, Mississippi, started its program in September 1977 and placed Dennis Kokaisel in charge of it. "It was a very successful program for us," he said."But initially it was a very difficult concept to sell to the workers. Our first circle was a pilot program that included fifty volunteers. By the end of the three-week training program we had lost ten people. They concluded it was too much work for them. One of the comments they made was, 'I'm not paid to take all this responsibility.' That is the real problem with dropouts. They are reluctant to take responsibility for their ideas."

Kokaisel learned six important facts after the pilot training was completed:

1. People must be trained to evaluate the job before and after their proposed changes have been instituted. This is difficult for blue-collar workers to accept. They have never before been asked what they would do to make their jobs better.

2. Many workers are willing to make suggestions. But the number who believe strongly enough in their ideas to analyze them and work to put them into effect is very small.

3. The company has to let workers try to solve their own problems. It can't use company troubleshooters to find solutions. The workers must do it all.

4. There are measurable results in departments where quality circles are active.

5. No company can expect to get 100 percent of the workers involved, but 80 percent is an excellent result.

6. The program will not cure all problems.

Sperry Vickers holds quality circle meetings weekly during regular working hours. Employees are paid their regular wages while in attendance. The meetings last one hour. Circle members do much of the work on their own time, as Kokaisel explained:

> The formal meetings identify the problem and find a solution to recommend to management. After the meeting, the members prepare charts, graphs, and other visual aids, organize their presentations, decide which members will speak about

the proposal, and get ready for the formal presentation to top management.

This is very exciting for workers who may never previously have spoken before any group, much less to the company president and vice-presidents. These circle members are experts in their subject areas. They cover just about everything from a change in machine design to the rearrangement of the workplace. They state what is wrong and how their solution will correct the problem.

Workers who have sold management on an idea can really be proud of themselves. They feel they control their lives and have a real voice in the management of the company. This feeling generates a desire to do the job even better.

MEASURING THE RESULTS
OF THE QUALITY CIRCLE METHOD

"Quality circles produce measurable results," Kokaisel said. "But other improvements don't translate into measurable dollar savings, simply because not all actions are judged by dollars in all areas." He went on to explain:

We find definite improvements in productivity where a circle is active. There have also been improvements in product quality. Also, once a circle is active in one department it creates interest in adjacent departments. Soon a circle forms there. We don't hurry the program along. We prefer to let the noninvolved workers see for themselves how the concept benefits others and let them take the first step to forming a group. Then we provide the necessary training.

Another unexpected benefit from the quality circle program appeared during labor contract negotiations. The information about the company's plans, which had to be discussed with quality circle members to enable them to do their work intelligently, provided the labor negotiators with a realistic picture of the company's financial condition. The facts helped to temper labor demands and produce an equitable contract.

No one claims that union people will proclaim you a hero for introducing the QC concept into your company. They may drag their feet or shoot down a proposal initially. But today's pull-together atmosphere seems much more conducive to such combined efforts at problem-solving than were the us-versus-them attitudes that marked the traditional union-management relationship.

QUALITY CIRCLES AT INTERNATIONAL HARVESTER

Management of the Solar Turbine Division of International Harvester in San Diego concluded late in 1976 that something had to be done to improve the quality of working life. The decision was not dictated by any major problem. The division was profitable and the product was of good quality. Employees were neither better nor worse than those of other firms in the area. The company simply decided that the quality of working life could be better and sought a method of improving it. Management decided to try the quality circle system. It set up a pilot program with Tom Erickson, director of organizational development and training, in charge.

Erickson's first step, after thorough study of the quality circle concept, was to make certain that top management clearly understood what was involved and that he would have full support, both financial and emotional. He explained:

> Most managements underestimate the difficulties involved in trying to introduce a concept as different as the quality circle into an established organization. At first, managers see the

circle as another tool to manipulate the worker into doing what they want. That concept is self-defeating. The quality circle is a new and quite disturbing way of life for everyone involved.

It is *not* a program that is imposed on the workers by management directive. The quality circle has none of the accoutrements of a program; there are no signs, banners, pep talks, or quotas. And there is no pressure for results. All those things, which are common in motivational efforts, are imposed on the workers by management and, for that reason, workers are suspicious of them.

To make the quality circle concept work, Erickson believes that management must offer six things: (1) good communication; (2) voluntary involvement; (3) a reward for participants; (4) recognition for participants; (5) a willingness to accept and implement the quality circles' ideas; and (6) consistency. Consistency means that the quality circle concept will continue along the lines established during the pilot program and not be subject to erratic changes dictated by someone's dissatisfaction with momentary results.

METHODS OF OPERATING QUALITY CIRCLES

Erickson sees the objective of the quality circle, from management's standpoint, as getting workers to do things as they should be done. This does not mean getting things done management's way; it means the best way. The quality circle concept declares that no one knows the best way better than the person who does the work.

"People cannot improve on the old ways of doing work unless they have time to consider what is wrong with things as they are," Erickson pointed out. "Therefore, you must provide time for circle members to meet without loss of pay. Circle members need to spend part of their working time gathering data. When the circle meets, you will find that people sometimes just sit and think. You wouldn't criticize a vice-president who sits in an office and thinks about a problem. So be patient when circle members do. Remember, this is a new experience for the workers. For the first time they have been asked to identify a problem, gather data, and offer a realistic solution. It's a tremendous change."

Erickson forbade industrial engineers from participating actively in the work of the quality circle. They could sit in as observers, but he did not want them to make suggestions. In the first place, they are members of management, and workers tend to bow to management suggestions. And in the second place, they do not understand the problems from the worker's point of view. This is similar, in essence, to the Japanese management concept where industrial engineers cannot impose job designs, though they do act in an advisory capacity.

"The initial training program is very important," Erickson declared. "You must first train the foreman to become a true leader. In the quality circle, there is no rank. The leader must do so by knowledge and force of personality. He or she must become an arbitrator, a teacher, and a synthesizer. Once you have trained the leader in the concept, you must get volunteers to participate. Then you must spend time training them in problem identification, data gathering and evaluation, and methods of presentation.

"We decided to form only two circles a month. Each one involves much work, training, rearranging schedules, and implementing proposals for change. To form more than two monthly would create too much work and confusion."

The quality circle should work within established organizational lines. For example, when the circle identifies a problem and devises a solution, it should make its recommendation first to the level of management that has immediate control. If that level is unreceptive, the circle should repeat its recommmendations to the next level. To do otherwise destroys lines of operational control and creates resentment and resistance.

THE ROLE OF THE FACILITATOR

A facilitator, who reports only to Erickson, sits in on each meeting of each quality circle. These facilitators are trained to moderate meetings and identify stumbling blocks. They do not actively participate in discussions, but when asked, they can provide advice and guidance. They also keep a record of what transpires in each meeting. Their role is similar to the one Estafen plays at Kaiser Permanente's group meetings. Management observers may attend meetings, but they cannot offer advice or criticism. After the quality circle has made a recommendation, the facilitator follows up to see that management implements the change.

"Implementation is vital," Erickson says. "If nothing happens, the circle members quickly see their effort as just a wasted exercise. They become demotivated. If it cannot take action, management must give the circle a detailed explanation."

The facilitator must never criticize or correct the quality circle leader in front of the group. If the leader needs suggestions or deserves criticism, the facilitator must offer them in private and as a teaching effort. Similarly, the circle leader must not attempt to dictate to other circle members during the meetings. Decisions are made by majority vote.

RESULTS OF THE QUALITY CIRCLE METHOD

In the first six months after the quality circles began to operate, definite results—some measurable, others not— were identified. For example, soon after the first two circles were organized, Erickson learned that there was a problem with scrap. The workers told him that few people understood why an article was scrapped, did not know what it cost, and did not know how to avoid the mistakes that created scrap.

"This was something management had just assumed everyone understood. So, the circle recommended we set up a scrap wagon. This was a display on wheels that moved around the plant so that people could see what makes a product unacceptable. On the cart we mounted examples of all our products, posted the cost of each, identified the things that made them scrap, and showed how to avoid them. There was a measurable reduction in scrap after the wagon started to roll."

As a nonmeasurable result, Erickson found that workers in departments where quality circles were organized were interested in what the circles were doing, even though they were not members.

The fact that circle members came around asking questions while gathering data made those people realize that someone was really listening to what they thought about their jobs. The nonmembers began to ask questions themselves. A lot of information was exchanged, to the benefit of both members and nonmembers.

"This is a healthy development," Erickson declared. "For example, a circle member will ask a nonmember about some job-related operation. That nonmember will bring up some experience from another job. The exchange of ideas that follows may produce a better way of doing some part of the work.

"People get pleasantly stimulated about this, and often nonmembers ask to become members after they have learned how the system works. We try to keep the circle to ten persons. If more want to join, we arrange for them to get into the next group. One department can have more than one group."

Another nonmeasurable result was one circle's solution to the problem of how to allocate labor costs to a large product that moved about the plant many times before it was shipped. Using a person to keep track of time was ineffective and created a false impression of cost. The quality circle made this recommendation: "Let's trust workers to keep track of the amount of time they spend on this product. Identify each product by number. Add up all time for that number, using the employees' time slips. Trust us to do it right." The solution worked.

COSTS AND SAVINGS
FROM CIRCLES

During the first six months of the program, four quality circles identified and solved problems. The cost of the time spent in meetings by the members was $8,000, and the savings realized was $90,000.

"Projecting a year ahead," Erickson said, "we estimated that each circle would cost us $4,000 and return $15,000. With twelve circles operating, we should expect to spend $48,000 and see a return of $192,000. We are very pleased with quality circles. Workers are voluntarily participating in decision-making. People are really interested in what they are doing. Workers are asking management, 'What does this cost?' And they are gaining an understanding of the limitations imposed by financial facts. We are convinced that the quality circle concept is a good answer to the old question, 'How do you get workers involved in doing their jobs the best way?'"

A QUALITY CIRCLE IN ACTION

Here is how a real QC meeting was conducted. This circle was composed of people from a number of departments. This particular area of the Solar Turbine Division at International Harvester is small and makes only one product, a complicated sheet-metal exhaust device that has many critical dimensions.

Represented at the meeting were people from inspection, shipping, inventory control, material movement, and sheet-metal layout, along with a foreman and a timekeeper. All were volunteers. A facilitator and an industrial engineer, as observer, were also present.

The group had met several times previously, and at its first meeting had focused on the problem of materials handling. At the early meetings, the circle discovered that completed exhaust manifolds were shelved for an average of four days before being moved to shipping. The company wanted to ship the manifolds as fast as possible because customers were waiting for them. The delay was costing thousands of dollars in cash flow and creating customer dissatisfaction. The problem: how to eliminate this delay.

During one meeting, the circle members presented the information they had gathered. They isolated several causes for the delay and presented facts to support their conclusions. Here are some of them:

1. Tow motors and forklifts that were used to move the exhaust manifolds were old and broke down frequently.

2. Inspectors were slow to put inspection tags on partially finished manifolds, resulting in parts sitting idle.

3. Inspectors did not inspect the initial layout of metal before the first process, resulting in errors and the need for extensive changes when finally discovered.

4. Tow motor operators mixed finished parts with unfinished parts because no marked space was set aside for completed manifolds.

5. Completed parts were not plainly labeled, and tow motor operators had to search for them to move them to the shipping department.

6. Completed manifolds were overlooked because of the lack of a specific place in which to keep them.

7. The shipping department failed to insist that completed parts be brought there promptly to be shipped.

8. Preventive maintenance on towmotors and forklifts was very poor.

9. There were not enough inspectors.

10. Forklift operators were not well trained, and they often damaged finished manifolds, causing delays for repair.

GETTING COMPLETE INFORMATION

As the discussion revolved around these causes, the foreman, as leader, kept asking, "Do we have enough information to prepare a solution?" At first, the members thought they had. However, as the discussion progressed, questions began to arise. Someone asked, "How many additional inspectors do we need?" No one had an answer. The foreman commented, "If we go to management with a request for more inspectors, the first thing they'll ask is 'How many?' We need to find out."

One person suggested that the company buy new forklifts and tow motors. Someone else asked how much they cost, but no one knew. The group agreed that one member should find out the costs.

There were suggestions to construct better racks for parts storage. Again the question of cost was unanswered. Said one participant, "If we are only going to recommend that the company spend money, we are wasting our time. The problem is organization, and cash isn't going to solve that."

Said another, "Training forklift operators to operate the lifts gently will save money."

Said another, "But training costs money, too."

The group became convinced that its members lacked enough information to make a presentation. They agreed that during the next week they would gather facts on costs and take a careful look at parts storage to see if the confusion could be solved without building shelves. They would ask the maintenance people to identify their problems with the lifts. They would request the shipping department to take a more active interest in matching finished parts with orders and to ship more quickly.

The facilitator then summed up the meeting and suggested that after the next meeting the group should be prepared to make a presentation and recommend action to management. The meeting lasted exactly one hour, though the foreman and facilitator remained behind for additional discussion.

QUALITY CIRCLES MOTIVATE THROUGH PARTICIPATION

The quality circle concept is an excellent method of obtaining worker participation in improving the quality of working life. Under ideal conditions it provides many of the needs identified by Maslow and the motivators mentioned by Herzberg. Participants gain recognition, assume responsibility, perform useful work, gain an understanding of how things really are in the industrial environment, and exert a positive influence on their own jobs.

A quality circle represents a long-term commitment by management, however. Several years may be required to prove conclusively that the concept is working. Management must also be willing to accept drastic changes in the way it manages its internal operations. In fact, control of the job and job content may become vested more in the worker than in the manager. This will be extremely disturbing to autocratic managers and supervisors and may indeed drive them out of the company. But that price may be worth paying if quality circles result in a highly motivated work force.

YOUR INVOLVEMENT IN QUALITY CIRCLES

Quality circles in 1984 do not enjoy the celebrity status they once did. There have been adaptations of the basic concept, and there have been failures. But the progressive manager should understand how the circles work. You may never come within a mile of a QC program at your firm. But then again, your next job may require that you know everything there is to know about this subject.

To give you a brief overview of the QC concept, some suggestions follow. Included are six initial errors to avoid, as well as a checklist of problems that could prove fatal to your motivation efforts in this area.

Don't memorize them. But think about them. One never knows. . . .

Pitfalls to Avoid In Setting Up QCs

There are a few things that you should *not* do when you introduce the QC concept:

1. Do not simply hand out written material and expect that alone to stimulate the workers' interest in quality circles.

2. Do not attempt to generate companywide enthusiasm all at once. Only one circle can be formed at a time. If many people volunteer at once all through the company, it will not be possible to accommodate them within a reasonable length of time. Initial enthusiasm will diminish, and resurrecting it will be difficult.

3. Do not accept more than ten volunteers for the first circle. Later, after the initial growth problems have been solved, a good leader may be able to handle a larger group. But too many too soon will create problems.

4. Do not fail to keep an accurate list of volunteers. When vacancies occur, take volunteers in the order in which they applied. Uneven administration of the program will create the impression that management doesn't really care.

5. Do not neglect to interview dropouts to find out why they quit. You may be able to pinpoint a personality conflict or a misunderstanding about the nature of circle activity and the requirements of membership.

6. Don't allow criticism, implied or actual, to be included in public statements. Things will go wrong from time to time, and they should be corrected promptly. But publicizing them is self-destructive. Always take the positive approach.

A Checklist of Potential Problems

Be on the lookout for any of these seemingly minor problems. Any one or combination of two or more could sabotage a firm's QC efforts.

( )   Not creating an implementation schedule

( )   Not obtaining management support

( )   Not keeping management informed

( )   Failure to involve *all* levels

( )   Incomplete operational guidelines or failure to establish them before the start of the pilot program

( )   Poor facilitators or group leaders

( )   Lack of support for facilitators and leaders

( )   Improper training

( )   Improper action by in-house consultants

( )   Poor group dynamics

( )   Employees in the program who are not volunteers

( )   Inadequate training materials

( ) Unpleasant atmosphere in meetings

( ) Indecision on management's part following a presentation

( ) Circles that become involved in matters outside their concern

( ) Leaders not giving top priority to scheduling of meetings

( ) Very authoritarian leaders who command instead of guide

( ) Management deciding who the volunteers will be

( ) Expanding the program too fast

( ) Failure to involve in-house consultants when they are needed

( ) Lack of involvement of nonmembers

( ) Unavailability of good meetingrooms

( ) Not considering normal problems that inhibit volunteer groups

( ) Not keeping support organizations advised of what's happening

( ) Management taking over circle problems

( ) Impatience among people in the program

( ) Facilitators getting too involved in content as opposed to process

( ) Poor recordkeeping

( ) Not setting goals and adhering to them

( ) Too much or too little publicity

( )   Postponing meetings

( )   Forgetting that this is a members' program

( )   Failure to implement accepted proposals properly

( )   Problems being resolved by quality circles outside their areas of skill

( )   Projects becoming too large

( )   Leaders unable to communicate feelings to facilitators for fear of reprisal

THE CASE OF MOTIVATION IN A NEW FACILITY

The ideal situation in which to introduce modern management techniques occurs when a new plant is constructed and a completely new work force is hired. A progressive management can then determine what style or system of managing it will use and introduce it to employees who understand it *before* they accept employment. This was the situation that existed at the polypropylene facility of Shell Canada in Sarnia, Ontario, when ground for the plant was broken in the late seventies.

You may never have such a prime opportunity yourself. But some of the ideas incorporated in this plant situation may be applicable if you open a new office or set up a new department in your firm.

THE APPROACH AT SHELL CANADA

Management of Shell Canada decided to discard the traditional system of dividing a plant into departments and the employees into groups under control of a foreman or supervisor, and confining each employee to a single task.

In its place, management created work teams of eighteen members, with one individual in each group designated as the coordinator. There were no supervisors or foremen in the plant. A special team was created to take care of special assignments that demand expert skills.

Each team consisted of employees who, taken all together, had the skills needed to run the plant. No one individual had any special assignment. When anything needed to be done, the team member closest at hand did it. If that person had difficulty, any member of the team who had a better understanding of the problem could provide assistance.

Work assignments were dictated by circumstances at any given time. A member might work one morning on a plumbing job and by afternoon be engaged in mixing a batch of chemicals. All employees underwent continuous training in a variety of skills. As the product of the plant changed, the new skills required would be taught.

Each team made many decisions that were formerly the prerogative of management. For example, team members arranged their own vacation schedules, meal periods, and daily work assignments. They also determined who needed training of what type and saw to it that those persons enrolled in the proper courses. Promotions and pay raises were based on ability, not seniority. Seniority came into play only if there was a layoff, something the company attempted to avoid.

The plant did not have any of the traditional status symbols such as executive dining rooms, preferential parking spaces, or corner offices. Management believed that such things served only to create two classes within the plant and to interfere with the free exchange of ideas.

Shell Canada's statement of philosophy said that the company's objective was to obtain an optimum return on investment in capital and human resources. At the same time it would operate a safe environment as a responsible member of the community, responsive both to the needs of employees and to the society in which it operated.

HOW MANAGEMENT AND UNION LEADERS FELT ABOUT THE TEAM APPROACH

Dick McFee, the initial operations manager at the plant, was especially pleased with the success of the new concept during the organizational phase. John Fisher, the first general manager, was also enthusiastic. He said, "We wanted to find a better way of doing work that would improve productivity and, at the same time, satisfy the needs of the individual. I do not believe it is possible to have high productivity without personal satisfaction with the job. What we created here is one of the most exciting things I have ever been involved in."

Union cooperation was absolutely necessary for the concept to succeed. Shell Canada made sure of this cooperation by recognizing the union as the bargaining agent even before ground was broken for the plant.

Stuart Sullivan, at that time the international representative for the Oil, Chemical and Atomic Workers Union, believed the plan would become a model for future plant organizations. But he cautioned that it was not transferable in its entirety to other types of industrial operations.

"What we created there was something special, designed to work well in the environment of a chemical plant," Sullivan explained:

We worked for eight months with Shell Canada executives to design a system that would work well for the Sarnia plant. They asked us to participate in work design and help create the system. We did that, and both sides were well satisfied with the results. The employees told me they were delighted with the way things were done. If any problems arose, I felt certain our good relationship with management would provide prompt solutions.

Under the new system there were no foremen or supervisors. The coordinator of each team was the liaison between the employees and the bargaining unit. The coordinator did not have the traditional hire-fire authority, and any disciplinary problems were to be handled within the group. Workers who were ineffective would get training. Lazy workers would be counseled by team members. We thought peer pressure to perform would be more effective than the traditional methods of discipline.

LABOR-MANAGEMENT COOPERATION AND MUTUAL TRUST

Sullivan and the Shell executives agreed that the biggest danger to the new plan was the traditionalists who refused to change. Some people, managers and workers as well, find themselves uncomfortable in a relatively unrestricted situation where decision-making is pushed down to the lowest level. Managers must accustom themselves to giving up much authority and learn to accept decisions made by workers.

The real key to success lies in trust between management and the work force. "It would have been impossible to negotiate our agreement unless we trusted one another," Sullivan said. "Trust is not something you can bring into existence overnight after years of not trusting. Trust comes from actions, not words. I think we developed a real trusting relationship in that case."

That trust was reflected in the collective bargaining agreement between Shell Canada and the union. In contrast to the usual huge, wordy contracts, this one fit into a small six-page booklet. There was no section dealing with management's rights. Seniority was covered in two short paragraphs that related only to layoffs. Grievances were covered in one paragraph. The wage schedule simply stated that there would be twelve grades and that raises would be based on achievement.

Improved management of the human resources of the company has provided all these organizations with an important means to forge ahead. While the methods used may differ in detail, a common thread runs through them: internal motivation. That is what you learned to measure in Part I of this book and how to inculcate in Part II.

Internal motivation springs from a number of sources. If one source could be singled out for its importance it would be *caring*, establishing a climate of trust between managers and workers. This factor appears to be present in all successful operations.

The concept of individual control also contributes to internal motivation. This concept gives workers more discretion about how to get their tasks done. Or, to look at it in another way, it removes unnecessary constraints on the workers in doing their jobs. The issue of flexible working hours, or flextime, is also a part of the individual-control concept.

New job designs that include horizontal or vertical loading also contribute to internal motivation. They increase responsibility, result in heightened self-esteem, and produce more motivated workers.

Teamwork and participation in problem-solving provide

internal motivation. Teams use effectively what one psychologist calls the most powerful motivator, the group. The support and reinforcement of team members, as well as the spirit of competition that teams often engender, result in increased performance.

Goal-setting at the worker or employee level has shown promise as a motivator. Several companies are experimenting with bringing the concept of Management by Objectives down below the level of supervisors and managers, with promising results in increased output.

These concepts can be employed by any organization to increase job satisfaction, improve quality of working life, and increase productivity with resultant benefits to companies and workers alike.

No one person or one book can provide you with the ultimate motivation system. Your own actions in this area will be as individualized as the other aspects of your personal management style. But by drawing on the experience of others, you can improve the way you motivate. In the end, that will make you a more successful manager.

INDEX

Absenteeism, 6, 9, 153
Administration of
  questionnaire, 26–29
Assembly line, 74
Attitude, defined, 10
Authoritarian style of
  management, 90
Autonomy, 76–77, 130–132

Benefits, 83
Benge Associates, 13, 16, 25,
  49, 57
Benton, Lewis, 7
Bureaucratic organizational
  structure, 78

Care, 71, 82, 140–141
Caring, 71, 82, 183
Catharsis, 95

Clerical level, motivation of,
  138–140, 142–153
Coercion, 72
Comeaux, Thomas, 8
Comments of employees, 49–
  52
Communication, motivation
  through, 82–84
Community relations, 57–58
Company policies, 83
Confidentiality, 27, 28, 51
Conflicting orders, 55, 56–57
Correspondence, secretary
  and, 120–121

Dalena, Donald, 71–72, 89
Deadwood employees, 91,
  95–99
Demotivation, 88–90

Departmental morale figures, comparison of, 40–43
Dewar, Donald, 161–162
Drucker, Peter, 5, 81, 149
Durkee, Richard, 144–147, 149–152

Eicher, Byron, 101, 102, 107
Empathetic listening, 94–95
Employee comments, 49–52
Employee councils, 57
Environment, 85–90, 136–137
Erickson, Tom, 165–170
Estafen, Bernard, 154–160, 168
Exit interview, 45–48

Failing subordinates, motivation of, 108–115
Favoritism, 89
Feedback, 71, 82, 77, 98
Filing, 121
Fisher, John, 181
Flextime, 130, 145–146, 183
Food for employees, 56
Freud, Sigmund, 95

General Motors Corp., 161
Groups, motivation of, 101–107
Growth, 98–99

Hall, Douglas, 6–7
Hendrickson, Caroline, 141

Herzberg, Frederick, 73, 80, 151, 174
Hewlett, William, 127–128
Hewlett-Packard, Inc., 127–141
Hinrichs, John, 8–9
Horizontal loading, 77, 183
HP Way, 217–241
Human Side of Enterprise, The (McGregor), 72

Incentives, 80–81, 89–90
Initial surveys, analysis of, 41, 44
Internal promotions, lack of, 53–55
International Association of Quality Circles, 161
International Business Machines (IBM) Corporation, 9, 11
International Harvester Company, 161, 165–173

Japan, 81, 161
Job design, 74, 76–77, 79, 183
Job enrichment, 59, 120
Job rotation, 79–80, 137
Job satisfaction, 58–59, 73
  defined, 10
  determination of potential for, 74, 75
  productivity and, 6, 7
Job security, 83, 129

Job Subordinate Worksheet, 109–114

Johnstone, Barbara, 140–141

Kaiser Permanente Medical Care Program, 154–160, 168

KITA (kick in the "pants" theory), 72

Kokaisel, Dennis, 162–164

Labor unions, 181–183

Lateness, 6

Lead persons, 133–134

Listening, empathetic, 94–95

Lowden, Tom, 129–134, 136–137

McClelland, David, 73

McDonald's Corporation, 79–80

McFee, Dick, 181

McGregor, Douglas, 72, 144

Management: Tasks, Responsibilities, Practices (Drucker), 5

Management actions, recommendations for, 61–65

Management by Objectives (MBO), 138–140, 144–149, 184

Management by Wandering Around (MBWA), 134–135

Management reorganization, 59

Management style, 3

Maslow, Abraham, 73, 80, 174

Mechanization, resistance to, 58

Monotony, 74

Motivating Economic Achievement (McClelland), 73

Morale:
  defined, 11
  productivity and, 6–7
  ways to study employee, 11–12
  See also Motivation; Questionnaires

Morale indices:
  analyzing data from, 36–48
  compiling, 35–37
  planning format, 30–31
  setting up tabulation, 31–35
  value of, 37–38

Morale surveys, 7–9, 11–12

Motivation:
  from coercion to, 72–74
  communication and, 82–84
  of deadwood employees, 91, 95–99
  environment, 85–90, 136–137

Motivation *(continued)*
of failing subordinates,
108–115
of groups, 101–107
HP Way, 127–141
job designs providing,
74, 76–77
Kaiser Permanente
Medical Care Program
and, 154–160
Management by
Objectives, 138–140,
144–149, 184
at new facility, 179–183
obstacles to, 77–81
Occidental Insurance
Company and, 142–
153
of professionals, 115–
118
psychotherapeutic
management and, 91–
95
quality circles, 161–178
of secretaries, 119–122
Shell Canada and, 179–
183
social responsibility as,
149–151
training as, 81–82, 133–
34
See also Morale;
Questionnaires
Motivation and Personality
(Maslow), 73

Motivation to Work, The
(Herzberg), 73
Multiple-choice questions, 15
Mutual need, 71–72, 82

Needs, 73, 80
New facility, motivation at,
179–183

Obstacles to motivation, 77–
81
Occidental Insurance
Company, 142–153
Open-ended questions, 14

Packard, David, 127, 128
Percentages:
analysis of findings and,
40
calculation of moral
indices in, 36–37
Position Planning, 140
Prestige, professional, 117–
118
Problem-solving supervision,
130–132
Professionals, motivation of,
115–118
Profit-sharing, 133
Promotions, 53–57, 89
Psychotherapeutic
management, 91–95

Quality circles, 161–178
Questionnaires, 6, 11

Questionnaires *(continued)*
　determining morale
　　through unsigned, 13–
　　25
　editing, 28–29
　for exit interview, 45–48
　morale indices. *See*
　　Morale indices
　techniques for
　　administering, 26–29

Report to employees, 65
Research, 3, 4
Responsibility, 77, 81, 151–
　152
Retirement, 56
Rewards, 80–81, 132–133
Rogers, Carl, 93, 95

Sabbatical leaves, 132–133
Salary, 51, 55–56, 83, 117
Sanzotta, Donald, 91
Sears Organizational Surveys,
　8, 11
Secretaries, motivation of,
　119–122
Self-actualization
　(fulfillment), 73, 80
Self-esteem, 93–94
Self-management, 99
Seniority, 89
Shell Canada, 179–183
Social relationships, 83
Social responsibility as
　motivation, 149–151

Solar Turbine Division of
　International Harvester,
　165–173
Sperry Vickers Division of
　Sperry Rand, Inc., 161,
　162–165
Strikes, 6
Subordinates, motivation of
　failing, 108–115
Sullivan, Stuart, 181–182
Supervision, 78
　conflicting, 55
　lack of, 55
　problem-solving, 130–
　　132
Supervision and Management
　(Benton), 7
Surveys, 7–9, 11–12.
　See also Questionnaires

Task advancement, 77
Taylor, Frederick W., 74
Team building, 102–104
Theory X, 72
Theory Y, 72–73, 144
Time clocks, 130, 146
Title of secretaries, 121–122
Training, 81–82, 133–134
Trust, 130, 144, 146, 182–
　183
Turnover, 6, 9, 153

Unsolvable problems, 57

Variety in jobs, 76–77, 99

Vertical loading, 77, 183

Wages, 51, 55–56, 83, 117
Walters, Roy W., &
  Associates, 74
Westinghouse Electric
  Corporation, 161

Whitney, Virgil, 116–
  118
Working conditions, 83,
  85–90
Work teams, 180, 182

Zenger, John, 78, 79